PROFILES

Jacqueline McLean

The Oliver Press, Inc.
Minneapolis

To my parents, who taught me to trust my wings.

The author and publisher wish to thank **Mary Sanford McLean** for the research and writing of Chapters 2 and 6.

The Oliver Press, Inc.
Charlotte Square
5707 West 36th Street
Minneapolis, MN 55416-2510

Library of Congress Cataloging-in-Publication Data

McLean, Jacqueline.
Women with wings / Jacqueline McLean
p. cm. — (Profiles)
Includes bibliographical references and index.
  Summary: Describes the lives and accomplishments of six famous women aviators: Harriet Quimby, Bessie Coleman, Amelia Earhart, Beryl Markham, Anne Morrow Lindbergh, and Jacqueline Cochran.
ISBN 1-881508-70-6 (library binding)
1. Women air pilots—Biography—Juvenile literature. 2. Women air pilots—United States—Biography—Juvenile literature. [1. Air pilots. 2. Women—Biography.] I. Title. II. Profiles (Minneapolis, Minn.)

TL539.M377 2001
629.13'092'2—dc21
[B]   99-086881
                                    CIP
                                    AC

ISBN 1-881508-70-6
Printed in the United States of America
07 06 05 04 03 02 01   8 7 6 5 4 3 2 1

Contents

*Although it lasted only a few moments, this historic
1910 flight by Blanche Stuart Scott—the first ever
piloted by an American woman—signaled the arrival
of women in the field of aviation.*

Introduction

On December 17, 1903, Orville and Wilbur Wright made the first sustained flights in an aircraft powered by an engine. From that moment on, aviation captured the hearts and imaginations of pilots-to-be everywhere. Despite the fact that early airplanes were unstable and accident-prone, flying seemed filled with romance. It promised adventure, freedom, and the dazzling opportunity to view the world from a different perspective. Daring pilots strove to fly longer, faster, and farther, each hoping to achieve another "first" in aviation.

Aviation was such a new and dangerous field that most people were shocked by the idea of a woman piloting an airplane. Men had been flying for five years before Mrs. Hart O. Berg became the first American woman even to ride in an airplane, making a two-minute flight as

Wilbur Wright's passenger. In 1910, Blanche Stuart Scott began taking flying lessons from the famous aviator Glenn Curtiss, but was not allowed to fly solo. Curtiss blocked the throttle so the airplane could not leave the ground during her lessons. One day, when Scott was practicing on the runway, she managed to take control of the throttle and brought the plane up about 40 feet into the air. With this short unofficial flight, she made history as the first American woman to fly an airplane.

That same year, a French woman named Elise de Laroche became the first woman ever to earn a pilot's license. Harriet Quimby, an ambitious and resourceful New York journalist, became America's first licensed

Elise de Laroche was already a well-known automobile racer when she earned her pilot's license. She flew successfully in several air races, but in 1919 became, tragically, the first woman to die in an air accident.

female flyer in August 1911. In her articles for *Leslie's Illustrated Weekly*, Quimby not only presented her readers with accounts of her adventures as a female pilot, but also encouraged them to get involved in aviation themselves. By the time Quimby won international recognition in 1912 as the first woman to fly across the English Channel, increasing numbers of European and American women were taking to the air.

During World War I, the need for new, fast, durable airplanes to fly in combat caused aircraft design to improve and production to increase dramatically. After the war, the U.S. government had more planes than it could use, so it sold its surplus to the public. For the first time in the history of aviation, pilots had access to affordable airplanes. But there were few jobs for the newly trained aviators returning from the war. To most people, aviation was still only an entertaining novelty; air mail was not widely used and commercial airlines had not yet been established. Many pilots in the 1920s had to make their livings as "barnstormers," independent flyers who traveled from place to place performing stunts in air shows.

A number of women achieved fame in the wild, glamorous world of barnstorming. Some made parachute jumps or walked on the wings of airplanes. Others climbed into flying airplanes from moving cars, or from one plane to another while soaring high above the ground. Still others were pilots, performing daredevil aerial acrobatics like loop-the-loops and barrel rolls. One

During her eight-year career as one of the many female barnstormers of the 1920s, Lillian Boyer performed stunts in 352 air shows.

of these pilots was Bessie Coleman, the first black American woman to earn her pilot's license. "Brave Bessie" thrilled audiences with each public appearance she made. For her, flying not only offered the opportunity to succeed as a woman, but also the chance to increase the self-esteem of other blacks. Coleman's short but inspiring career fueled many dreams.

In 1929, the Fédération Aéronautique Internationale (the international organization governing aviation) established a category to recognize women's record flights. Setting records for speed, distance, endurance, and altitude allowed female pilots to demonstrate their skills and gain recognition for their achievements. That same year, women also entered competitive racing. Nineteen female pilots flew in the First Women's Air Derby, and by the mid-1930s, women were competing in races that previously had been open only to men. Races and record-setting helped women in aviation meet and support one another, creating a sense of community. There were about 200 licensed female pilots in America in 1930; five years later, the number had grown to almost 800.

Amelia Earhart—perhaps the most famous woman aviator—built her career on racing, record-breaking, and other daring feats in the 1930s. Among her many landmark achievements, she was the first woman to cross the Atlantic Ocean by air. Earhart considered aviation to be a tremendous opportunity for women to prove their equality with men. "Women must try to do things as men have tried," she once said. "When they fail, their failure must be but a challenge to others." Earhart mysteriously disappeared in 1937 while attempting to fly around the world at the equator—something no man or woman had ever tried—but her legacy of courage survived.

For many women pilots, aviation was becoming more than a daredevil hobby. The career of Beryl Markham, a British woman raised in Kenya, demonstrated the potential professional uses of aviation. As the only female commercial pilot in East Africa at the time, Markham flew a total of a quarter of a million miles over difficult terrain, delivering mail and supplies, bringing doctors into remote areas, and acting as a courier for safaris. Known for her self-reliance and endurance, Markham described flying as "my job."

During the 1930s, many aviators worked hard to prove that flying could be a safe, convenient mode of transportation for ordinary people. Women aviators played a central role in popularizing the fledgling commercial airline industry. For instance, Anne Morrow Lindbergh explored airline routes around the world as the copilot for her famous husband, Charles Lindbergh.

Because women were thought to be timid and delicate, they were often used to highlight the "safety and reliability" of aviation in advertisements like this one.

Together, the Lindberghs flew thousands of miles to plan the most secure and practical routes for commercial airlines. To people who believed women were weaker than men, the fact that shy, sensitive Anne endured these flights proved that air travel could be safe for everyone.

Anne found beauty and peace in flying, and wrote about her love for aviation in her books, diaries, and letters. Once, as she and Charles took off from North Haven Island, Maine, in their airplane, Anne looked down at the landscape of her childhood summer home and wrote: "The island falling away under us as we rose in the air lay still and perfect, cut out in starched clarity against a dark sea. I had the keenest satisfaction in embracing it all with my eye. It was mine as though I held it, an apple in my hand." When she was flying, the world seemed to belong to her.

In the 1940s, World War II brought new opportunities for women who loved flying. Although they were forbidden to join the military, women took over jobs as airplane factory workers, flight instructors, air traffic controllers, and mechanics when the men in those jobs were needed to fight in combat. Seeing a desperate need for pilots to help with the war effort, Jacqueline Cochran organized and directed the Women's Air Force Service Pilots (WASP), an elite corps of female pilots trained to fly military aircraft. Cochran took tremendous pride in her work, becoming a vocal advocate of women's equality with men in the air. Members of the WASP ferried and

The more **WOMEN** at work
the sooner we **WIN!**

*Women's contributions in industrial jobs such as
airplane building were essential during World War II.*

tested planes for the U.S. Army Air Force and performed
many other important duties.

After the war, Cochran continued her career as a
respected pilot, flying competitively and breaking records
in the most sophisticated aircraft. She became one of
the first women to pilot a jet plane and, in 1953, the first
woman to fly faster than the speed of sound. Cochran was
less successful, however, in her fight to convince the
United States government to recognize the WASP as part
of the military. Most people expected women to leave the
jobs they had performed during the war and return to
their roles as wives, mothers, and homemakers.

Despite opposition, however, women continued to make advances in the field of aviation. In fact, women flying today have more options than ever before, including flying in the military and working as commercial airline pilots. Patty Wagstaff—perhaps one of the most famous modern women pilots—is an aerobatic pilot and six-time member of the U.S. aerobatic team. The liberation Wagstaff experiences in the air echoes the spirit of women aviators who came before her. "Aviation," she has said, "just symbolized everything that I loved. It was freedom, total freedom. You can get in an airplane, you can leave, you can go somewhere else, and you can be up there all by yourself. You grab hold of the stick in the plane and everything is sort of right. The world's at peace."

Women With Wings looks at the history of aviation as it is encapsulated in the lives of an extraordinary group of women who flew during the pioneering days of flight. For some, the peace and beauty they experienced in the air were compelling reasons to fly. For others, flying represented freedom, a way to assert their autonomy. Some women were driven by the need to prove their equality with men, while others were lured by the promise of undiscovered frontiers. Flying is about all these things, but for the early women aviators and many women flying today, it has also been about perseverance and strength of character. As pilot Judith Chisholm has said, "All it takes is determination, an independent spirit and a thick skin."

With her pioneering career as a pilot and her skill as a journalist, Harriet Quimby (1875-1912) was the first to show the world that women could make their mark in the field of aviation.

1

Harriet Quimby
America's First Woman of the Air

On the morning of August 1, 1911, Harriet Quimby made her second attempt at the exam for a pilot's license. She felt both excited and nervous as she began her test flight, but she took the plane up smoothly. Then, just 20 feet up in the air, a gust of wind suddenly hit the left wing, tipping the plane to the right. Staying calm, Quimby managed to bring the plane back under control. As she rose to an altitude of 150 feet, her confidence increased. The plane reached a speed of 45 miles per hour, and Quimby executed the first of the five turns the test required. Once again, the wind tilted the plane dangerously, this time to the left. If Quimby did not correct the balance, the plane could stall and fall to the ground. Still, she did not lose her composure, and brought the plane level again.

After Quimby made the last of her turns and performed five figure eights, she prepared for the final part of the flight test: the landing. Taking aim at the white square on the field that marked her touchdown spot, she began to drop in altitude. When the plane was six feet off

Just before taking her pilot's exam, Harriet Quimby (standing, right) receives last-minute instructions from her teacher, Andre Houpert (kneeling, center).

the ground, Quimby pulled back on the lever and the wheels touched down perfectly. She counted to three and then flipped the switch that shut down the engine. Soon, all she could hear was the creaking of the wood frame as the plane bounced along the grass landing strip and came to a stop. She knew she had flown well.

"After the flight," Quimby recalled, "I removed my goggles, then climbed out of my monoplane and nonchalantly walked over to the two official observers sitting on wooden chairs beside the flight line. I looked one of them in the eye and said, 'Well I guess I get my license.' 'I guess you do,' the official replied." And with that, Harriet Quimby became the first American woman to earn a pilot's license. She was the thirty-seventh person and only the second woman in the world to do so.

Harriet Quimby was born in Coldwater, Michigan, on May 11, 1875, to William and Ursula Quimby. In 1884, nine-year-old Harriet, her parents, and her older sister, Kitty, moved to Arroyo Grande, California, a farming community not far from San Francisco. The small farm they purchased quickly failed, however, and William worked odd jobs to make ends meet.

The family's economic situation did not improve until Ursula Quimby took charge. She did not want her daughters to be dependent on men for their survival, nor did she want them to do backbreaking farm work. Ursula convinced her husband to move to San Francisco, where there were better jobs and a more stable economy. There,

Ursula put the family to work for her brother, who was famous for his herbal medicines. She and her daughters mixed and bottled the remedies while William traveled around selling them from a wagon. Ursula and the girls also made sacks for the local fruit-packing industry, and the extra income enabled Kitty and Harriet to attend good schools in the city.

Despite Ursula's hopes that both her daughters would become independent, Kitty soon married. After Kitty left home, the determined mother channeled all her dreams into Harriet. It was Ursula Quimby who created the mystery that came to surround her daughter's background. Ursula wanted people to believe that Harriet was the child of a prominent and wealthy family. She invented a story to perpetuate this illusion—that Harriet had been born in Boston and educated in Switzerland and France. In addition, she claimed that Harriet had been born in 1884, making her nine years younger than she really was. Ursula believed that an image as a young, well-educated, and affluent woman would give Harriet an extra edge in the male-dominated society of the early 1900s.

Intelligent and determined, Harriet Quimby could succeed on her own merit. She decided to be a journalist, a career that was becoming increasingly open to women. By 1901, she had found work as a reporter for the *San Francisco Dramatic Review*, and soon she also began writing for the Sunday edition of the *Call-Bulletin & Chronicle*. She worked hard, looking for stories throughout the city.

The editor at the *Chronicle* quickly recognized the young reporter's abilities, saying she had the "best nose for news" he had ever seen. By 1902, Quimby was one of the *Chronicle*'s star writers, and her byline had become well known throughout northern California.

Always drawn to new challenges, Quimby decided to try to make a name for herself on the East Coast. On a wintry day in January 1903, she arrived at Pennsylvania Station in New York City. As she stepped outside onto the dirty, bustling streets, she realized that building a career in New York was going to be a real challenge.

The editors for the New York papers were tough, and skeptical of female reporters. Not one to be dissuaded, Quimby eventually convinced the editor at *Leslie's Illustrated Weekly* to give her a year's trial. In an early piece for *Leslie's*, she stressed the value of perseverance in trying to succeed in New York. "With a fund of humor," she advised her readers, "and a wholesome but not surplus quantity of courage, you will in time rejoice that you came; for while competition is keen, it is also an incentive."

Quimby's own perseverance paid off. With her interest in America's melting pot culture and other social issues, the young reporter more than proved herself to the editor of *Leslie's*. By 1906, Quimby was the paper's drama critic and the editor of the Women's Page. She also became the first travel correspondent for *Leslie's*, journeying to South America and Africa. At a time when it was still rare for women to use mechanical devices,

Quimby learned to use both a typewriter and a camera in the course of her job. She then became fascinated by automobiles. She obtained her driver's license, bought her own car, and encouraged her female readers to learn to drive. "Automobiles have opened up a new world for women," she wrote.

Quimby was also attracted to the new world of aviation. In the autumn of 1910, her friend Matilde Moisant invited her to an air show at Belmont Park on Long Island. Quimby was so intrigued by what she saw that she

Matilde Moisant (left) and Harriet Quimby became close friends who encouraged each other's interest in aviation.

John Moisant was a flamboyant and self-promoting pilot who designed airplanes, managed a flight school, and founded America's first flying circus, the Moisant International Aviators.

became determined to try flying herself. She approached Matilde's brother, John Moisant, about taking lessons at his flying school. Though John agreed to teach both Quimby and his sister to fly, he said that they would have to wait until spring to begin their training.

The two women did begin flying lessons in the spring, but John Moisant was not their instructor. In December, he had been killed in an airplane crash. Such accidents happened frequently during the early years of aviation, and they made flying highly controversial. Women were especially discouraged from flying because they were considered weaker and less courageous than men. Yet neither Quimby nor Matilde Moisant was dissuaded. So as not to attract attention, they disguised themselves as men and began their lessons in secret.

When a *New York Times* reporter blew her cover, Quimby decided to capitalize on the sudden publicity. She convinced her editor to have *Leslie's* sponsor her as a pilot. That way, she could write about her flying experiences and the paper could increase its readership. *Leslie's* quickly agreed to the proposition, and Quimby began writing a series of articles on aviation, the first of which appeared on May 25, 1911. It was entitled "How a Woman Learns to Fly."

During the early years of flight schools, students spent little time in the air. Their first week of training included lectures on flight theory and the basic structure of the airplane. In the second week, students familiarized themselves with planes by taking them apart and reassembling them. During the third week, students took turns climbing into a plane that had been bolted to the hangar floor. While still on the ground, they could feel the power of the engine as they moved the controls, learning to react to different flight situations.

Only during the fourth week did students begin to operate a moving plane. Their biggest challenge involved learning to guide the plane in a straight line over a grass

*Harriet Quimby learned to fly at one of the few pilots'
schools that accepted female students, the Moisant
School of Aviation in Hempstead, New York.*

strip. After mastering this process, students tried making
the plane hop up in the air two or three feet at a time, a
technique called "kangarooing." Finally, during the fifth
week, came the most important lesson: the supervised
solo. Those who completed short flights successfully
could then take the pilot's exam.

Quimby had finished 33 lessons and had spent
barely two hours in the air when her instructor, Andre
Houpert, told her she was ready for the exam. On July
31, 1911, Quimby successfully completed the first two
parts of the exam, but did not pass the landing test. A

pilot was required to land within 100 feet of the spot where the plane had left the ground, and Quimby landed too far away. The next day, however, she succeeded. And how! Quimby landed only seven feet and nine inches from the point of takeoff.

Despite the common prejudice against women pilots, Quimby had earned her license without a single accident in the air. Furthermore, observers said she had made the most precise landing that had yet been made, and she had set a new student altitude record. Twelve days later, Matilde Moisant also passed her exam, becoming America's second licensed female pilot.

Strange as it sounds, Quimby's first challenge as a pilot involved what to wear while flying. Since there was no precedent for women's flying gear, Quimby had improvised an outfit out of pieces of men's clothing. Some *Leslie's* readers found this get-up inappropriate for a woman pilot. Yet traditional women's clothing of the time—long skirts and blouses covering tightly corseted waists—made flying nearly impossible. In the end, Quimby asked a New York tailor to make her a flying costume. Alexander Green came up with a stunning one-piece outfit made of purple satin, with full knickers that reached below the knee.

Once she had earned her license, Quimby began to promote aviation as a growing industry in which women could play an important part. "I see no reason the aero-plane should not open a fruitful occupation for women,"

Harriet Quimby in her famous purple satin flying outfit, the bottom half of which could be converted into a skirt. High-laced black boots, a hood, flying goggles, driving gloves, and a long cape completed the ensemble.

she wrote. "I see no reason they cannot realize handsome incomes by carrying passengers between adjacent towns, from parcel delivery, taking photographs or conducting schools of flying." Though some manufacturers refused to sell an airplane to a woman, Quimby used her connection with the Moisant school to buy a 50-horsepower monoplane. John and Alfred Moisant had successfully copied this light, reliable plane after one designed by the French aviator Louis Blériot.

Before long, Quimby began flying at air meets. On September 4, 1911, she flew over Staten Island and became the first woman to make a night flight. "It was grand," she said. "I did not feel like ever coming to earth again." Quimby's flights continued to give her material to write about, and her aviation articles were so popular that every issue of *Leslie's* that carried one sold out.

The greatest challenge of Quimby's career proved to be her attempt to fly across the English Channel. If all went well, she would be the first female pilot to make the flight between England and France, and *Leslie's* would have exclusive rights to the story. To ensure that she would be the first, Quimby kept her plan a secret.

On March 7, 1912, Quimby sailed for Europe. In France, she met with Louis Blériot, who was not only an airplane designer but also one of the few men who had successfully flown the Channel. Quimby bought a new Blériot 70-horsepower monoplane, but discovered it would not be ready for several weeks. So she would not waste precious time, Blériot lent her his own 50-horse-power model for the Channel crossing. Quimby wanted to take the plane for a trial run before her flight, but the weather did not cooperate. After several anxious days of waiting, she decided to go ahead without a trial flight. She traveled to England, and the plane was secretly shipped across the Channel.

*On July 25, 1909, Louis Blériot (1872-1936),
French monoplane designer and pilot, became the first
person to fly across the English Channel.*

Sunday, April 14, 1912, brought clear weather. Quimby and her friends drove to the aerodrome outside of Dover. Across the Channel, they could see the French town of Calais, which lay just 22 miles away. Conditions were perfect and her friends urged her to go ahead with the flight, but Quimby refused. She had promised her mother not to fly on a Sunday under any circumstances.

Monday brought clouds, rain, and gusting winds over the Channel, so Quimby was delayed again. "I was eager to get into my seat and be off," she later wrote.

"My heart was not in my mouth. I felt impatient to realize the project on which I was determined. . . . For the first time I was to make a journey across the water."

On Tuesday, conditions had improved. Pilot Gustav Hamel, who had made the Channel crossing three times, checked out the plane, and Quimby prepared for takeoff.

As Harriet Quimby prepares to take off on her flight across the English Channel, Gustav Hamel (standing on plane) makes a final check of the aircraft.

She was airborne by 5:30 A.M. "On takeoff," Quimby recalled, "I saw at once that I had only to rise in my machine, fix my eyes upon Dover Castle, fly over it and speed directly across to the French coast." Hamel gave Quimby a compass for the flight, and though she had never used one before, she followed its needle accurately and kept on course. After one hour and nine minutes of exhausting concentration, she landed on a French beach.

Quimby was welcomed by a crowd of very surprised French fishermen who gave her breakfast right there on the seashore. "These humble fisherfolk knew the significance of what had happened," she wrote in her column. "They were congratulating themselves that the first woman to pilot an airplane across the Channel had landed on their fishing beach." Reporters and photographers from the *London Daily Mirror* arrived to document the record crossing, and they drank a champagne toast to Quimby while she posed for photographs in her airplane.

Quimby anticipated a warm welcome back in the United States, but it didn't happen. Two days before her flight, the White Star liner *Titanic* struck an iceberg in the North Atlantic and sank into the black waters. More than 1,500 people were killed in the most terrible sea disaster the world had ever known. The tragedy of the *Titanic* totally eclipsed Quimby's dramatic flight.

Still, Quimby knew she was establishing a solid reputation for herself as a skilled aviator. That summer, she was billed as "America's First Lady of the Air" at the

Boston Air Meet. As the event's main attraction, she would be paid $100,000.

On July 1, 1912, the second day of the meet, Quimby set out to break the overwater speed record of 58 miles per hour that had been set the year before by an English pilot. William P. Willard, the manager of the air meet, would accompany her on a 27-mile course over Boston Harbor, around a lighthouse, and back, while the crowd watched breathlessly.

The outbound flight went well. Then, as Quimby made her turn around the lighthouse to head back to the field, the plane's tail rose sharply. The sudden movement hurled Willard out of the plane. He was seated behind Quimby, so she was not immediately aware of what had happened. Realizing that her balance had shifted, she tried to pull the nose of the plane up. Just as it seemed the plane was responding to her command, the tail suddenly pitched upward again, turning the plane perpendicular to the water. This time, Quimby was thrown from her seat. On the ground, horrified spectators watched as first Willard and then Quimby tumbled into the harbor waters, 200 feet from shore. Willard drowned, and Quimby died on impact.

There were dozens of theories about the cause of Quimby's accident. Some people blamed the designer and mechanic of the airplane she had been flying. Others pointed out that neither Quimby nor her passenger had been wearing seat belts, although few aviators did so at the

After Harriet Quimby's fatal crash, spectators pull the wreckage of her plane from the ocean.

time. Many people used her death to argue that women were not physically or psychologically fit to be pilots. But despite her tragic end at the age of 37, Harriet Quimby remains one of aviation's heroes. Just before her death she had received a permit from the United States Post Office that would have made her the first woman to fly the mail. This accomplishment was just one sign that Quimby was a true pioneer, using her skills as a writer and her abilities as a pilot to ensure American women a role in the future of flight.

Before taking off in the thrilling, dangerous world of stunt flying, Bessie Coleman (1892-1926) had to fly in the face of prejudice that denied black women the opportunity to become pilots.

2

Bessie Coleman
No Prejudice in the Sky

*A*s the horrified crowd in the Checkerboard Aerodrome watched, Bessie Coleman hurtled downward in a Curtiss airplane. It looked as if she had lost control of the plane and would crash straight into the ground. But just 200 feet above the runway, the nose of the plane began to rise. After pulling out of her nosedive, Coleman soared back into the sky, circled the airfield once, and made a perfectly smooth landing. The entire maneuver had been a daring stunt.

Once on firm ground, Coleman was greeted by cheers and a check for $1,000 from the organizers of the air show. She had performed barrel rolls, loop-the-loops, and figure eights for amazed family members, friends, and admirers at what is now Midway Airport in Chicago. It was October 15, 1922, and Coleman had come a long way from her three-room childhood home in a small town in Texas. With her winnings, she was flying toward her ultimate goal: opening an aviation school for anyone who wanted to learn to fly.

But reaching her goal was much like aviation itself—sometimes easy and fun, sometimes bumpy and dangerous. In the 1920s, women were still discouraged from having careers outside the home. Bessie Coleman had other obstacles to face, as well. The United States was strictly segregated, and black Americans like her did not have the same opportunities as whites.

Born to Susan and George Coleman on January 26, 1892, Bessie was the sixth of nine surviving children. In the early years of Bessie's life, her father made a meager living as a day laborer in the cotton fields that surrounded the family's home in Waxahachie, Texas. But when Bessie was six years old, George decided to seek a better life in Indian Territory (now the state of Oklahoma). Because he was both African American and Native American, George was doubly discriminated against in Texas. In Indian Territory, his Native American ancestry would entitle him to the full rights of citizenship. When Bessie's mother protested that she did not want a rough pioneer life for her children, George left his family behind.

To support herself and the four of her children who were still at home, Susan Coleman worked as a maid for a white family. Once a year during the harvest, all the Colemans picked cotton in the fields. Bessie was a bright child who used her talent in mathematics to make sure that the foreman did not cheat her family out of their earnings. Although she often missed school to care for her younger sisters while her mother worked, Bessie gained confidence from taking on adult tasks. And she always dreamed of doing something special with her life.

After graduating from the town's one-room school-house in 1910, Bessie attended the Colored Agricultural and Normal University in Langston, Oklahoma. Paying for her education with money she had earned while working as a laundress, Bessie was able to afford only one term at the school. But she was in college long enough to do a research paper on Orville and Wilbur Wright, the brothers who invented the airplane.

Back at home, Bessie was restless. There were few opportunities in Waxahachie for women who did not marry. But Bessie had a plan. When her older brother Walter invited her to live with him in Chicago, she worked for three years doing laundry and cleaning until she saved enough money to go. At the age of 23, Bessie Coleman took her seat in the shabby black section of the segregated train bound for Chicago.

From 1910 to 1920, Chicago, like many other northern cities, was a popular destination for southern blacks looking for job opportunities. The city offered Coleman a whole new world of people and experiences. After settling into Walter's apartment, she spent time in an area known as "The Stroll"—eight blocks along State Street on Chicago's mostly black South Side. There, she soon found a job working as a manicurist at the White Sox Barber Shop.

One day when Coleman was working in the barbershop, her older brother John, recently back from World War I, visited her. He bragged about the women he met in France during the war. John said that French women were beautiful and independent, and some could even fly airplanes. That comment struck Coleman. "That's it. You just called it for me," she told John. Suddenly she knew what she wanted to do: she would learn to fly.

But how could she get started? Coleman had heard of women flyers like Harriet Quimby, and of black aviators like Eugene Bullard, who learned to fly in France during the war. But she had never heard of a black female pilot, because there weren't any.

Well then, Coleman thought, she'd be the first. She asked aviation teachers in Chicago to teach her, but no one would take her on. Some told her they believed women should not be flying because it was too dangerous. But she suspected their refusal might also have been because she was black.

Robert Sengstacke Abbott (1870-1940) founded the Chicago Defender *in 1905. Read by thousands, the newspaper was largely responsible for the migration of southern blacks to northern cities.*

One of the barbershop patrons was Robert Abbott, the influential editor of a black weekly newspaper called the *Chicago Defender*. Coleman thought he could help her. One day, while manicuring Abbott's nails, she told him about her dream. Abbott said he would look into possibilities for her. He was interested in "uplifting the Race," he said, and helping Coleman become a pilot would be a way to prove what African Americans could accomplish. This was the beginning of an important alliance between Bessie Coleman and Robert Abbott.

Abbott soon located a school in France that would teach Coleman to fly. She worked on her French, applied for a passport, and got a job in a chili parlor where she could make more money to save for her trip. Her family worried about her desire to fly, but they had realized long before that she liked to do things her own way.

In December 1920, Coleman started her flying course at the École d'Aviation des Frères Caudron in Le Crotoy, a part of France near the English Channel. She took lessons for seven months, learning to fly in a French Nieuport Type 82 biplane. In this plane, a teacher would sit in the front seat, working the controls, and a student pilot sat in the back seat. From there, the student could not always see the instructor, or hear him over the roar of the engine. Students learned by feeling the movements of the controls and mimicking the instructor's motions.

On June 15, 1921, at the age of 29, Bessie Coleman received her license from the Fédération Aéronautique Internationale. She was the first black woman in the world to earn a pilot's license. When Coleman returned to the United States in September, reporters from both black and white newspapers were waiting to interview her. She was also the guest of honor at *Shuffle Along*, a popular Broadway musical with an all-black cast. During the intermission, the famous performers presented Coleman with a silver cup.

On the train ride from New York back to Chicago, Coleman planned her future. She remembered how hard it had been for her to find someone to teach her to fly and thought about how she wanted, in Robert Abbott's words, to "uplift the Race." Then it struck her: she would open an aviation school to teach more blacks how to fly. In an interview for the *Chicago Defender*, she explained, "We must have aviators if we are to keep up with the times. I shall never be satisfied until we have men of the Race who can fly. Do you know you have never lived until you have flown?"

Coleman knew that to pursue her flight school dream she would have to make some money. But in the 1920s, there were no commercial airlines to hire pilots. Some licensed pilots worked for the postal service, but almost all of them were white men. Many pilots could only make a living as entertainers. They would "storm" the countryside, looking for opportunities to perform at air shows. They often made impromptu performances in open fields and slept in nearby barns at night. Thus, these adventurous aviators were known as "barnstormers."

In order to be a barnstormer, Coleman would have to learn some flight stunts. In air shows, pilots did loop-the-loops and barrel rolls, turning their planes upside down or around and around. Some pilots had performers walk on the wings of their plane or asked passengers to parachute out. Coleman had not learned any of these stunts during her flight training. She knew she would have to take more lessons, so she returned to France in February 1922.

Coleman trained in France for two months and in Germany for 10 weeks. She met European aviators, talked to German plane manufacturers about buying a plane, and even was filmed flying over Berlin. The world was becoming aware of Bessie Coleman.

In her aerial exhibitions, Bessie Coleman wore a tailored military-style uniform.

When Coleman returned to the United States in August, reporters again rushed to interview the new celebrity. Not wasting any time, Robert Abbott arranged an air show in Long Island that would feature Coleman. Although the people who loaned her a plane to fly did not allow her to perform stunts there, Coleman was still the star of the show. On September 3, a large crowd turned out to see the first public flight of a black woman in America.

This air show was followed a month later by the Checkerboard Aerodrome show in Chicago. Because of her thrilling stunts, Coleman was crowned "Queen Bess, Daredevil Aviatrix" and "Brave Bessie." She became a heroine in Chicago and many people wanted to fly as her passenger or simply meet her. A beautiful, intelligent, and confident woman, Coleman was well suited for her fame.

Soon after the Checkerboard Aerodrome show, the African American Seminole Film Producing Company wanted Coleman to star in a movie loosely based on her experiences. Coleman signed a contract, went to New York, and began work on the film, which was called *Shadow and Sunshine*. On her first day, however, the script called for her to dress in rags as a poor, uneducated southern black girl coming to New York. Coleman did not like the way the script depicted her background or black women in general, so she walked off the set, refusing to play the role. She wanted to help her race, and she felt that this movie made blacks look unsophisticated and ignorant.

Unfortunately, Coleman's decision alienated many powerful men in the black entertainment world. With few supporters, no sponsor, and no plane of her own, Coleman had to find money fast. She made an alliance with the Coast Tire and Rubber Company in Oakland, California. If she would drop advertisements for them from an airplane, they would buy her a plane. Coleman went to Oakland to meet with the company and then traveled down to Los Angeles to arrange an air show.

By February 4, 1923, Coleman was ready for the show, in which she would fly her own plane—a Curtiss JN-4, known as a Jenny. Although this Jenny was a new plane to Coleman, it was actually an old plane left over from World War I. Shortly after taking off for the show, the motor stalled and the plane fell 300 feet to the ground. Coleman was seriously injured, breaking one leg, fracturing several ribs, and suffering internal injuries. Outraged that they hadn't seen the show they had been promised, the crowd demanded their money back. The crash was a major setback for Coleman and for her career. Not only was her recovery long and difficult, but her plane was also destroyed. She was not discouraged, however, and in a telegram to friends she said: "Tell them all that as soon as I can walk I'm going to fly!"

Returning to Chicago without any money, Coleman started planning a series of lectures and air shows in Texas. This southern tour was a great success. In borrowed planes, Coleman flew daringly in shows and lectured in

The Curtiss "Jenny" was the primary training craft for American pilots during World War I. Sold off at bargain prices after the war, Jennys were popular among struggling barnstormers like Bessie Coleman.

Houston, San Antonio, Dallas, and even her home town of Waxahachie. To generate more income, she also gave rides to excited spectators. She made enough money to cover her expenses and saved the rest for her school. In Dallas, Coleman made a down payment on another Jenny, planning to save money to pay for it later. She returned to Chicago at the end of 1925, full of confidence.

HERE SOON!

Aviatrix Bessie Coleman

In Person and on the Screen with 2000 Feet of Film Showing her Flights in Europe and America.

Read the Following Facts About the Dashing and Daring Girl who Flirts with Death in Her Airplane.

She is a Ranch Girl.

Born in Texas.

She weighs 130 lbs.

She is a graduate of the French School of Aviation at Paris, France.

She is the only woman in the world that handles a 22 horsepower German Benz Plane and she flew over the palace of the Ex. Kaiser, in Berlin, Germany, with a Pathe Camera Man.

She is the only woman in the world holding an international Pilots license, enabling her to make flights in any country.

An advertisement for one of Bessie Coleman's many public appearances

46

After a brief visit with her family, who she always missed when she was on the road, Coleman left for a tour of the southeast. Her lectures at churches, schools, and theaters in Georgia and Florida were well attended. Children gathered around Coleman admiringly after each of her appearances, and her talks inspired many blacks to learn to fly. In Orlando, she stayed with Reverend Hezekiah Hill from the Mount Zion Missionary Baptist Institutional Church and his wife, Viola, who was active in the community. Coleman joined their church and grew close to the family, who shared her mission to "uplift the Race." Coleman also met Edwin M. Beeman, the heir to the Beeman chewing-gum fortune. Beeman helped her pay the remaining debt on the Jenny plane she had ordered in Dallas.

In late April 1926, Coleman arranged for a young white pilot and mechanic, William D. Wills, to fly her new plane from Dallas to Jacksonville, Florida, where she was planning to perform in an air show. The plane had engine problems during the journey, forcing Wills to make two emergency landings in Mississippi. He reached Jacksonville safely, but the plane needed some work. Again, this plane was new to Coleman, but it was far from being new. She simply had to make do with the aircraft that fit her budget.

After working on the plane, Wills told Coleman that it was ready to fly. On the morning of April 30, Wills and Coleman took off from Paxon Field to fly over the racetrack where the air show would take place the next day. Wills flew the plane so Coleman could survey the flight space from the back seat. She left her seat belt unbuckled so she could lean over the side of the plane to see.

Wills and Coleman flew to the racetrack and circled the area. Once they had seen the field, they rose to 3,500 feet and headed back to Paxon Field. The plane was cruising at 80 miles per hour when suddenly it nose-dived, jumping to 110 miles per hour. At 1,000 feet, the plane went into a tailspin. When the plane flipped over at 500 feet, Coleman was thrown out. She tumbled to the earth and was killed by her fall.

Wills, trying unsuccessfully to regain control of the plane, crashed into a field over 1,000 feet away from Coleman's body. Wills survived the crash, but bystanders could not free him from the plane. When a representative from the Negro Welfare League reached the site, he lit a cigarette to calm his nerves and accidentally set the plane on fire. Wills died in the blaze.

Mourners flocked to memorial services for Coleman in Jacksonville and Orlando, and then Viola Hill accompanied her friend's body back home. At a service at the Pilgrim Baptist Church in Chicago, an estimated 15,000 people came to say farewell before Bessie Coleman was buried in Lincoln Cemetery.

Investigators later discovered that the accident had been caused by a wrench left in the engine that had jammed in the gears. This would never have happened with a

The Elite Circle and Girls DeLuxe Club
expect you and your friends to enjoy
"An Aerial Frolic"
honoring
Miss Bessie Coleman
Sat. May 1, 8:30 to 12 P. M.   Pythian Auditorium
Subscription 75c
Music by the Imperial Jazz Orchestra

*An invitation to the dance that was to be held in
Bessie Coleman's honor on May 1, 1926, after her
performance in the Jacksonville air show. Coleman
was killed on April 30, however, and instead of the
"Aerial Frolic" they had expected, admirers attended
her funeral.*

newer plane, in which the gears would have been covered. But the old Jenny was the best that Coleman could afford.

In white newspapers of the time, Coleman's accomplishments were nearly ignored. Articles about the crash focused on Wills, saying he was "teaching Bessie how to fly." Coleman's air show appearances and lecture tours were never mentioned, and she was often referred to as "the Coleman woman" or simply "the woman." But a reporter for the *Chicago Defender* wrote, "Though with the crashing of the plane, life ceased for Bessie Coleman,

Bessie Coleman's dreams lived on in the career of her nephew Arthur W. Freeman, who was inspired to become a pilot after watching her perform in an air show when he was eight years old.

enough members of the race [have] been inspired by her courage to carry on in the field of aviation. . . . Whatever is accomplished by members of the race in aviation will stand as a memorial to Miss Coleman."

As the reporter predicted, Coleman's dreams did not die with her. In 1977, a group of black women who were student pilots founded the Bessie Coleman Aviators Club. In 1990, a road at Chicago's O'Hare Airport was renamed Bessie Coleman Drive, and in 1992 Chicago's mayor declared May 2 Bessie Coleman Day. Every year on the anniversary of Coleman's death, black pilots fly over her grave and drop flowers in tribute.

In his eulogy for Coleman, Junius C. Austin commented, "this girl was 100 years ahead of the race she loved so well." Bessie Coleman not only found a way to fly in a nation that refused to teach black women to become pilots, but she also endeavored to make her dream available to others. As she once said, "The sky is the only place there is no prejudice. Up there, everyone is equal. Everyone is free."

"It may not all be plain sailing," Amelia Earhart (1897-1937) once said of aviation, "but the fun of it is worth the price." During the course of her career, Earhart experienced both the rewards and the penalties of fame and flying.

52

3

Amelia Earhart
The Maverick

"*A*ren't you excited?" a reporter asked Amelia
Earhart after she, pilot Wilmer Stultz, and mechanic Lou
Gordon completed their flight from the United States to
England on an airplane called the *Friendship*.

"Excited?" she replied. "No, I was just baggage."

"You're still the first woman to fly the Atlantic."

"Oh, well," Earhart said, "maybe someday I'll try it
alone."

It was June 1928, and Earhart, at 30 years of age,
had just become the first woman to cross the Atlantic by

air. Bill Stultz had flown the plane, but it was the daring Earhart who captivated the world. Tall and lean with a tousled mop of blonde hair and a maverick's grin, she closely resembled another aviation hero—Charles Lindbergh, the first person to fly solo across the Atlantic Ocean. Like Lindbergh, "Lady Lindy" would use her fame to show that flying could be a safe and practical means of transportation. But another goal also defined Earhart's career: proving that women could be good professional pilots.

Amelia Earhart was both idealistic and independent, qualities she displayed even as a young child. Born on July 24, 1897, in Atchison, Kansas, Amelia scorned "girls' games," preferring to invent her own. Once, after seeing a roller coaster at the St. Louis World's Fair, she decided to build one herself. Propping planks against the roof of a tool shed in her backyard, the seven-year-old built a ramp that she could coast down on a cart. She had several crash landings, but declared the ride was "just like flying."

Amelia's parents encouraged her adventures. Her mother, Amy, had been the first woman to climb Pike's Peak in Colorado. Amelia's father, Edwin, was a kind man, although he gradually sank into alcoholism as Amelia grew older. As his career in railroad law became more unstable, the family relocated so frequently that Amelia attended six high schools in four years. With little opportunity to make friends, she grew into a self-reliant young woman. Amelia Earhart was determined to make a

At about the age of seven, Amelia Earhart (right) poses with her younger sister, Muriel, on the front porch of their home in Kansas City.

difference in the world, despite society's confining view of women's roles. Believing women should share in all life's opportunities, she resolved to go after her goals. For inspiration, she filled a scrapbook with newspaper clippings about women who had built successful careers in unconventional professions.

Earhart's passion for aviation began on a Los Angeles airfield in December 1920 when she persuaded her father to buy her a ticket for a flight with pilot Frank Hawks. "As soon as we left the ground, I knew I myself had to fly," she said. Earhart studied with a female pilot named Neta Snook, and later learned aerial acrobatics with an ex-army flier and movie stuntman, John "Monte" Montijo. As her love of flight increased, so did her appreciation of the airplane as a machine, and she learned to repair aircraft as well.

In 1921, Earhart earned her pilot's license from the National Aeronautic Association. For her 24th birthday, she used her savings to purchase her first plane: a small used Kinner Airster biplane, which she named *Canary* for its yellow color. In her new plane, she flew to 14,000 feet and set a new women's altitude record. By 1923, when she received her Fédération Aéronautique Internationale flying certificate—which allowed her to make attempts on world records—Earhart was already making a name for herself.

Yet flying was expensive, and Earhart had to support herself through a variety of odd jobs, including driving a gravel truck. In 1925, she found a position as a social worker at Denison Settlement House in Boston. There, she cared for the needs of Chinese, Armenian, and Syrian immigrants. Earhart played with the children, visited their impoverished homes, and taught them English. The job brought her a great sense of accomplishment, for she knew she was making an important difference in people's lives. But she spent her weekends flying.

It was while Earhart was at Denison that former army captain Hilton Railey and publicity wizard George Palmer Putnam contacted her about the *Friendship* flight.

The plane's wealthy owner, Amy Phipps Guest, wanted to sponsor a record-setting flight, and she had hired Railey and Putnam to find "the right sort of American girl" to become the first woman to cross the Atlantic Ocean by air. The charming and intelligent Earhart was perfect for the role. She would only be an unpaid passenger, but accomplishing this "first" could bring her fame and other aviation opportunities. Sure enough, after the June 17 flight, Amelia Earhart was on her way to becoming a legend

Amelia Earhart, Wilmer Stultz (right), and Louis Gordon are welcomed home with a parade in New York after their historic flight on the Friendship.

in her own time. As a legend, she would constantly test her limits, and the stakes would keep getting higher.

For the next year, Earhart traveled around the country giving interviews, lecturing, and making publicity appearances. With the help of Putnam, who had begun managing her career, she published a book about her flight on the *Friendship*, wrote a monthly aviation column for *Cosmopolitan* magazine, and endorsed merchandise from flying suits to automobiles. Earhart began to realize that she could make a career as an aviator, and also that she could play a vital role in promoting air travel. She worked to publicize Transcontinental Air Transport, one of the first commercial airlines. And in all her public activities Earhart advocated the safety and practicality of aviation, aiming her message particularly at women.

Earhart not only encouraged women to be airline passengers, but strove to support female pilots as well. Since women were not allowed to participate in men's flying races, she helped organize a cross-country race for women. In August 1929, she and 18 other female pilots flew from Santa Monica, California, to Cleveland, Ohio, in the First Women's Air Derby. After the race, Earhart and pilot Ruth Nichols started a women's flying association that still exists today. Called the Ninety-Nines, it was named for its 99 charter members. Earhart served as the organization's first president.

On February 7, 1931, Earhart married G. P. Putnam. She had thought she would never want to marry, and in

G. P. Putnam and Amelia Earhart were not only husband and wife, but also a strong publicity team that worked tirelessly to advance Earhart's career.

fact Putnam had proposed six times before she said yes. Putnam's ability to raise funds for her projects probably played a role in Earhart's decision to enter the union, which she referred to as "an attractive cage." All the same, husband and wife seemed to love each other sincerely. Most important to Earhart, Putnam respected her fierce need for independence. In fact, he encouraged her to pursue increasingly daring flights.

Four years after the *Friendship* crossing, Earhart felt she had yet to prove herself as an aviator on a par with Charles Lindbergh. She was driven by the need to demonstrate that women were the equals of men, and once wrote to her husband, "Women must try to do things as men have tried. When they fail, their failure must be but a challenge to others." In 1932, she decided to establish herself as a first-class flier by becoming the first woman to fly solo across the Atlantic Ocean.

On May 20, 1932, the fifth anniversary of Charles Lindbergh's legendary Atlantic crossing, Earhart took off from Harbor Grace, Newfoundland, in her Lockheed Vega. For the first few hours of her flight, she encountered good weather and flew at 12,000 feet. Then flames began shooting from the exhaust system. Her altimeter, the instrument that records altitude, failed. Earhart ran into a violent lightning storm and was driven off course. Hoping to pull out of it, she climbed higher for half an hour, only to realize that she had hit freezing rain. The ice weighted down the plane, covered the windshield, and caused the airspeed indicator to malfunction. Suddenly, the Vega went into a spin, dropping so low that Earhart saw the ocean waves breaking below her before she regained control.

For the next 10 hours, Earhart fought to stay low enough to prevent icing but high enough to use her remaining instruments, which would not function properly in lower altitudes. The warmth of the air soon melted the ice, and she was able to regain control. "Probably if I had been able to see what was happening on the outside during the night I would have had heart failure then and there, but, as I could not see, I carried on," she remembered.

Come morning, Earhart was horrified to discover a fuel leak. Her fuel gauge was broken, so she had no idea how much fuel was left. And if the fuel reached the burning exhaust system, the plane would explode. She had to give up her plan to fly Lindbergh's course to Paris and find a place to land. Turning the Vega northward, Earhart eventually came down in a cow pasture in Ireland. "I've come from America," she called to the farmer who watched her land. He exclaimed in shock, "Holy Mother of God!"

Even though she hadn't reached Paris, Earhart's flight time was 14 hours and 56 minutes—the fastest transatlantic crossing yet. After this record journey, Earhart once again found herself the center of intense publicity. She was not only the first woman to pilot a plane across the Atlantic, but also the first person since Lindbergh to have made the flight alone and the first person to cross the Atlantic twice by air. President Herbert Hoover awarded Earhart with a gold medal from the National Geographic Society, making her its first female recipient. She was also awarded the Distinguished Flying Cross by the Army Air Corps. Always an advocate for women, Earhart wrote that one of her motives in making the flight was to prove that "women can do most things men can do, . . . jobs

Amelia Earhart poses for photographers in the Irish cow pasture where she ended her transatlantic flight.

requiring intelligence, coordination, speed, coolness, and will power."

Although Earhart's crossing earned her the respect of the world, there was a huge price to be paid. Her friend Walter Trumble predicted the dark side of Earhart's fame: "Probably never again can Amelia Earhart walk on the streets of any city [like] an ordinary citizen. She will be pushed and tugged and ever surrounded by the maddening throng."

Nevertheless, Earhart refused to be overwhelmed by fame, and she soon channeled her restless energy into new projects. On August 24 and 25, 1932, she broke the women's transcontinental speed record, flying from Los Angeles to Newark, New Jersey, in 19 hours and 5 minutes, the longest continuous time she had ever flown alone. On that same flight, she also set a women's record for distance—2,447 miles. A year later, she tried again and shaved nearly two hours off her own record time.

By the age of 37, Earhart had already set nine records in 12 years and was known as "The Queen of the Air." Yet she continued to go after new challenges. During the fall of 1934, she set to work on her next project: a 2,400-mile flight from Honolulu to California, over the longest open stretch of water anywhere in the world. No one had yet soloed successfully over any part of the Pacific, and Earhart knew that she was the one to do it.

She hired Paul Mantz, a stunt pilot and engineer, to overhaul the Vega for the trip. Mantz brought the Vega's fuel capacity up to 470 gallons of gasoline and 56 gallons of oil. In the cockpit, Mantz checked the existing navigational equipment and installed some new instruments, including compasses and an ice-warning thermometer. A pilot's skill, Earhart knew, was not the only component necessary to break records. The plane, too, had to be equal to the challenge.

By January, both Earhart and the Vega were ready. She took off from Honolulu on January 11, 1935, in exceptionally bad weather, and brought the plane up to 5,000 feet in an attempt to reach clear skies. Still, she encountered clouds and almost continuous fog. This was blind flying in the truest sense of the word. But after 17 hours and 7 minutes, Earhart touched down safely in Oakland, California.

With this flight, Earhart became the first person to fly from Honolulu to California, the first person to solo

Crowds of fans surround Amelia Earhart's plane in Oakland, California, after her flight across the Pacific from Hawaii.

over the Pacific, and the first person to solo over both the Atlantic and Pacific oceans. In crossing such a vast expanse of water, Earhart proved that people could fly anywhere in the world. Her flight helped make possible the growth of Pacific air travel.

After conquering the Pacific, Earhart accepted a job as an advisor in aeronautics at Purdue University in West Lafayette, Indiana. There, she acted as a career consultant for female students. Meanwhile, the Purdue Research Foundation set up a fund for the purchase of a new, more sophisticated plane for her use. In this Lockheed Electra, Earhart planned to go after her most daring record yet. She would fly around the world at the equator—something no man or woman had ever tried.

The world flight was Earhart's idea, but it was G. P. Putnam who set about arranging permits, licenses, and landing fields around the world, as well as campaigning for funding and publicity. Putnam also worked with Paul Mantz to make the plane flightworthy. Clarence Belinn, chief engineer for National Airways, designed a cross-feed system for 10 gasoline tanks in the body and wings, with a master valve in the cockpit floor. The tanks gave the plane a flying range of 2,500 to 3,000 miles, enough to cross long stretches of water without refueling. By the time work on the Electra was completed, the plane would be worth $80,000—approximately $1.5 million today.

Once Mantz and Belinn set to work on the plane, Putnam tackled the publicity. He wanted the public to

Amelia Earhart with her Lockheed Electra

feel they were watching history happen in this unprecedented flight, but it would not be easy to capture attention in a time of national economic depression and political instability abroad. In the end, Putnam advertised the Electra as a "flying laboratory" in which Earhart planned to study "human reactions to flying." With this message, he hoped the world would be fascinated by Earhart's journey. He was right.

The Electra was ready at the end of July 1936, and Earhart spent the next five weeks learning all she could about it. She was impatient to make the journey, a fact that worried Mantz. He tried to persuade his friend to spend more actual flight time in the plane before undertaking such a dangerous trek, but Earhart did not take his advice. She couldn't; she was too busy raising money to pay for the phenomenally expensive trip. And she was eager to be off.

With Fred Noonan, an experienced navigator, Earhart launched her flight westward from California on March 17, 1937. Almost immediately, she suffered a setback when an ominous and mysterious accident occurred. During takeoff in Hawaii on March 20, the Electra crashed

Paul Mantz (left), Amelia Earhart, and Fred Noonan (far right) in Hawaii before launching Earhart's around-the-world flight

on the runway like "a poor battered bird with broken wings," as Earhart described it. No one knew what happened, but they were grateful that the plane had not burst into flames. While the Electra was being repaired, Earhart decided to reverse her flight route and fly eastward from Miami. There, on June 1, Earhart and Noonan climbed into the Electra's cockpit and took off.

Earhart flew about 22,000 miles in the 32 days that followed, stopping to rest and refuel at airports along the way. She and Noonan traveled along the northeast coast of South America, then across the South Atlantic, Africa, and southern Asia to Australia and New Guinea. They encountered severe weather, including monsoon rains over the Bay of Bengal. The plane took such a beating that it had to be entirely overhauled by KLM Airlines in Java.

Earhart and Noonan were also feeling the strain of the journey. For a month, they had endured a rigorous schedule of long flights, takeoffs and landings in all conditions, and endless publicity appearances. Earhart was always up before 4 A.M. to prepare the details of the next legs of the trip—supervising maintenance, studying flight maps and weather reports, and dealing with reporters and customs officials. She suffered from dysentery, an intestinal tract infection that causes severe nausea and diarrhea. Although she had dreamed of this incredible flight, she was physically and mentally exhausted by it. Worse yet, the hardest part of the journey still lay ahead.

At 10 A.M. on July 2, Earhart and Noonan left Lae, New Guinea, in a nerve-wracking takeoff. They were now facing the most dangerous and demanding part of the trip: the 2,500-mile flight to Howland Island, a sandbar in the mid-Pacific that is only two miles long and three-quarters of a mile wide, with a maximum elevation of 25 feet. The tiny island would be extremely hard to find from the air.

Based on the position she radioed to Lae at 5:20 P.M., Earhart stayed on course and covered about one-third of the distance to Howland Island during the first seven hours of the flight. But later that night, when the U.S. Coast Guard ship *Itasca* (which was stationed near Howland Island) radioed Earhart to ask for her position and anticipated arrival time, she didn't answer.

The *Itasca* regained contact with Earhart at 3:45 A.M., and her voice came in faintly several times during the next five hours. The ship's commander, however, knew he had an emergency on his hands. Earhart must be off course and unable to locate Howland Island. All she reported was, "Gas is running low . . . we are circling."

At 8:44 A.M. on July 3, 1937, listeners aboard the *Itasca* heard Earhart say, "We are running north and south." She sounded breathless and confused. This was the last message ever heard from Amelia Earhart. Twenty-one days before her 40th birthday, she disappeared—just a few flights short of completing her journey around the world. Although the area surrounding Howland Island

Amelia Earhart's puzzling disappearance was front-page news for weeks, and investigations into the circumstances of her death continue to this day.

was searched extensively, neither the Electra nor the bodies of Earhart and Noonan were ever found.

"When I go," Earhart once said, "I would like to go in my plane. Quickly." In the end, she apparently got her wish, although to this day the circumstances of her death remain a mystery. But the legendary aviator has lived on in the imaginations of people everywhere. "Pilots are always dreaming dreams," she said. Earhart not only dreamed, but she also gave the world something to dream about.

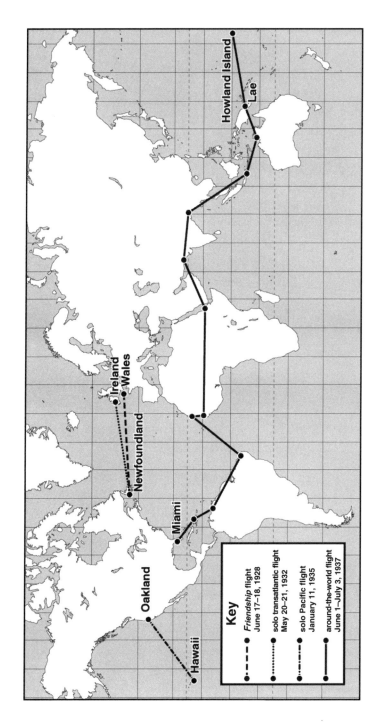

Amelia Earhart's major flights

"*The advent of airplanes seemed to open up a new life for us,*" *Beryl Markham (1902-1986) once wrote.* "*The urge was strong in me to become a part of that life, make it my life.*" *In doing so, she built a career as a commercial pilot and captured the world's attention with her adventures.*

4

Beryl Markham
Heroine from Africa

O n September 5, 1936, Beryl Markham's airplane crashed nose first into a bog in Nova Scotia, Canada. Markham managed to walk away from the crash unhurt, except for a bad bruising and a gash on her forehead. After climbing out of the cockpit and surveying the damaged plane, Markham trudged three miles through the waist-high mud until at last she met up with two fishermen. The fishermen took one look at the exhausted, bleeding aviator and then took her to the nearest farmhouse and called the local doctor.

Beryl Markham's historic flight from England to North America ended with an emergency landing that buried the nose of her airplane six feet deep in this swamp.

Markham had not made it to New York as planned, but she had achieved her goal. After braving bad weather for 21 hours, she had become the first woman to cross the Atlantic the hard way, flying east to west against powerful headwinds. The Atlantic crossing proved to be Markham's first and last attempt at a record. Though she loved a good challenge, Markham was not particularly interested in publicity stunts. "Flying is my job," she said. "It is no romantic adventure, but a hard job of work." Yet flying was a job she loved.

Markham was born Beryl Clutterbuck in Leicester, England, on October 26, 1902. Two years later, her family emigrated to East Africa. The area was controlled by the British government, and settlers like the Clutterbucks were drawn there with promises of cheap land and potential fortune. Beryl's father, Charles, established timber mills and a farm at Njoro, about 80 miles north of Nairobi, Kenya.

Although the family's enterprises were successful, Beryl's mother, Clara, found settler life lonely and difficult. When Beryl was four, Clara returned to England permanently with Beryl's older brother, Richard, who was too sickly to withstand the African climate. Eventually, when Beryl was a teenager, her parents divorced. Never forgetting her mother's abandonment, Beryl remained wary of women all her life. She became devoted to her adventurous father, an avid horse breeder. From him, Beryl inherited her energy and her passion for horses. When Beryl was in her teens, she helped deliver her first foal, which she named Pegasus for the flying horse in Greek mythology.

As Beryl grew, so did her love for Africa. The house at Njoro looked out on the majestic Aberdare mountains on one side, and onto brilliant blue-green forests full of leopards and other wild animals on the other. Growing up in these surroundings, Beryl never lacked for adventure. Her best friend, Kibii, was the son of a Nandi tribesman who worked on the farm. Kibii's father taught both children how to handle a spear and shoot with a bow and arrow. From him, the strong and agile girl learned courage. She didn't know it yet, but her African childhood would prove excellent training for her career as an aviator.

Beryl grew into a self-reliant young woman who possessed qualities of both African and British cultures. She learned to speak the languages of the peoples of the region—Swahili, Nandi, and Masai. Eagerly, she listened to native legends, finding them far more interesting than the nursery tales imported from England. From the Africans, Beryl learned to respect self-control and bravery. Yet Beryl was also British, and she had frequent contact with the upper-class British settlers in East Africa. When she chose, she could fit easily into high society, displaying cultured manners and speech.

Life on the farm at Njoro passed uneventfully until 1919, a summer of disastrous drought. Charles Clutterbuck lost all he had, and Beryl suddenly found herself forced to make her own way in the world. She tried marriage, first to the Scottish rugby player Alexander "Jock" Purves and later, in 1927, to the English aristocrat Mansfield Markham. Yet Beryl Markham was far too free-spirited to play the traditional wife. After giving birth to her son, Gervase, in 1929, she sent him to live with her mother-in-law in England and saw him—and Mansfield—only infrequently.

She stayed in Africa, successfully earning a living by training racehorses.

Then in the autumn of 1929, when Markham was 27 years old, she discovered the magic of flying. The man who introduced Markham to flight was a charismatic Englishman, Denys Finch Hatton. Markham admired Finch Hatton and soon fell deeply in love with him. After a few rides in his airplane, she was determined to learn to fly herself. That spring, she began flying lessons with an ambitious professional pilot named Tom Campbell Black.

At the time, East Africa was ripe for the arrival of the airplane. Because the terrain was rough and there were

Denys Finch Hatton (1887-1931), one of the most well known big-game hunters of his day, shared Beryl Markham's passion for Africa and introduced her to the thrill of flying.

few roads, airplanes were able to reach places automobiles could not. Planes delivered cargo and ferried passengers to remote areas of the country. This was no easy feat in East Africa, where altitudes were often high, maps were poor, and runways were dirt tracks full of holes, anthills, and sometimes wild animals. Although aviation was often the most convenient mode of transportation in the wilderness, flying under such conditions was highly dangerous. On May 14, 1931, Denys Finch Hatton was killed in his airplane while taking off from Voi in southeastern Kenya. In that area, the hilly terrain and hot weather created strong downward currents of air, one of which had struck Finch Hatton's plane and sent it spinning out of control until it crashed and burst into flames.

Although Markham was devastated by Finch Hatton's death, she was even more determined to become a skilled pilot. Just two months after the tragedy, she earned her pilot's license and then immediately began studying for her "B" license, which would allow her to become a commercial pilot like Tom Black. For this examination, she needed to be able to strip and clean an engine, as well as understand the theory and practice of navigation. On September 18, 1933, Markham passed the exam and became Kenya's first female commercial pilot. "My girl, you are getting somewhere at last," she said to herself.

After earning her commercial license and buying her first plane, Markham took any flying opportunity that came her way. In just three years, she flew more than a quarter of a million miles over dangerous territory. One of her first jobs was delivering mail and supplies to miners at the East African gold mines of Kakamega, Musoma, and Watende. Flying to these regions was extremely difficult. "The airstrips," said Markham, "were pocket handkerchief size and a forced landing anywhere en route meant almost certain death from thirst." Markham's other jobs included providing air taxi service to settlers in remote areas, delivering doctors and medical supplies in emergencies, and flying accident victims or seriously ill patients to a hospital in Nairobi. In addition, Markham was one of the first commercial pilots to scout game for safari hunters. Flying high overhead, she could locate elephant herds and direct the hunting party toward them.

Markham's career as Kenya's only female commercial pilot in the 1930s was enough to ensure her a place of honor as a pioneer aviator. Still, the ever-adventurous Markham continued to go after new challenges. Not only did she log 250,000 miles as a freelance pilot, but she also flew great distances solo. One of Markham's major journeys was the 6,500-mile trip from Kenya to England— which she made six times, four of them solo. For her, the most memorable of these trips was in March 1936, when she set off north from Kenya in a Leopard Moth airplane with the famous game hunter Bror Blixen as her passenger. As she noted, "It was not a record flight either in speed or endurance . . . but it was not a dull flight."

At the time, flights between Nairobi and London were rare, and the terrain was considered so dangerous that no woman was allowed to fly alone over the Sudan without the permission of England's Royal Air Force. In southern Sudan lay vast papyrus swamps where a forced landing would be incredibly difficult and the chances of being rescued were next to zero. Beyond the swamps stretched 3,000 miles of barren desert.

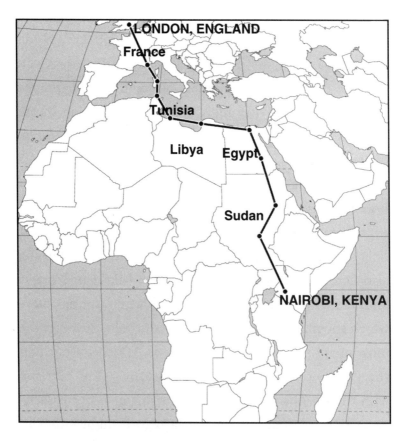

Beryl Markham's route from Kenya to England

When Markham and Blixen reached North Africa, which at the time was occupied by the troops of Italian dictator Benito Mussolini, they met further challenges. In Egypt and Libya, they were detained by Italian officials who accused Markham of being both a spy and a man in disguise. It was the eve of World War II, and the Italians were afraid that Markham was taking stock of their military from the air. When she and Blixen were finally allowed to take off over the Mediterranean Sea, they encountered winds of 60 miles per hour and driving rain that made it impossible to see. Markham had to bring the plane up to 10,000 feet before she reached blue sky again. After a stop in Paris to rest and refuel, the Leopard Moth touched down in England the following afternoon.

While Markham was in London, her wealthy acquaintance John Carberry made her a tempting proposal. He said that if she would attempt to fly nonstop from England to New York, he would give her the use of his brand new airplane, a Vega Gull. Markham knew that Amelia Earhart was the only woman to have flown the Atlantic solo, and she had done it the "easy" way, from west to east. Many aviators had made unsuccessful attempts to fly the east-west route across the Atlantic, which was more difficult because it required a pilot to fly against powerful winds. But Markham, who loved a dare, needed no time to consider Carberry's offer. She had been longing to go after one of the distance records for quite some time. Carberry's offer of the Gull, then under construction, made Markham's longing a reality.

The Gull, which Markham named *The Messenger*, was due to be ready in August. The plane was specially designed to fly long distances. The body was longer and wider than standard models, and it had been custom fitted with extra fuel tanks: two in the wings, two in the center section, and two more in the cabin. This gave it a total capacity of 225 gallons and enabled a pilot to fly about 3,800 miles without refueling. For a nonstop ocean crossing, this increased fuel capacity was essential.

Markham spent the summer training. She exercised to build her stamina and pored over maps, studying the routes and plans of both successful and unsuccessful Atlantic crossings. The aviator Jim Mollison helped Beryl plan her trip. Mollison was the one person to have made an east-west flight, but he had started from Ireland, completing the ocean crossing in only 19 hours by flying to Newfoundland, the shortest route.

On September 4, 1936, Markham was ready to take off. The media had hyped her coming flight. Headlines ran the bold statements: ATLANTIC HOLDS NO TERRORS FOR FLYING WOMAN and DARE-DEVIL SOCIETY WOMAN LEAVES TODAY. But Markham downplayed her gender and social class. "I . . . fail to see what an accident of birth has to do with flying the ocean," she wrote coolly in an open letter published in a London newspaper the day after she took off.

82

Mollison and Edgar Percival, the plane's designer, accompanied Markham to a military runway in Abingdon in central England. The ground was covered with puddles from a morning rain. Just before Markham climbed into the cabin, Mollison said, "Luck, Beryl. You deserve the best." At that moment, Markham knew she needed all the luck she could get. The runway was a mile long, and with a 1,900-pound load of gasoline, the plane would need every inch of that runway to lift off. There was a possibility that the heavy plane wouldn't become airborne. But Markham got *The Messenger* off the ground in just 600 yards.

Once she was airborne, however, visibility proved so bad that Markham flew blind for 19 hours, relying on her instruments to see her through. Yet her two greatest challenges were fatigue and loneliness. The journey required incredible concentration—especially given the bad weather. *The Messenger* had never been fitted with a radio, so Markham knew that if she ran into trouble, she couldn't even call for rescue. People wouldn't know where to begin to look for her. Alone in the air, these thoughts preyed on her mind.

Markham flew against strong headwinds, longing for her first sight of land. Suddenly, one of her fuel tanks ran dry and the engine died. *The Messenger* dropped hundreds of feet before fuel from a new tank reached the engine. This tank was her final one, and its gauge said it would last 11 hours. But only 9 hours later, the engine began to fail again. "I watched that tank getting emptier and emptier and still saw nothing but sea and clouds and mist," Markham later wrote. Finally, just as the engine stopped, she sighted land. She made an expert landing in a nearby field, only to discover that what she had taken for grassy ground was really a moss-covered bog. *The Messenger* plowed down into the peat just 300 feet from the water's edge and tipped up on its nose. Markham struck the windshield and lost consciousness.

Beryl Markham soon after her transatlantic flight, her forehead still bandaged from the crash landing

Markham later discovered that ice had choked the flow of fuel to the carburetor, causing the engine to die. She had landed at Baleine Cove on the northeast coast of Nova Scotia, after flying an exhausting 2,212 miles in 21 hours and 35 minutes. Despite her initial fears of failure, she had succeeded in becoming the first person to make a solo nonstop flight from England to North America and the first woman to fly the Atlantic from east to west. Though she had not made it to New York City, she had crossed the Atlantic the hard way.

Markham's triumph, however, was dimmed by her discovery that her mentor, Tom Campbell Black, had been killed in a bizarre airplane crash in Liverpool. On September 18, while he was moving down the runway to take off, another plane landed on top of his; its propeller sliced through the roof of the cabin and into his shoulder and lung. Markham was horrified that Black, the most careful and skilled pilot she knew, could have met his death in what the press called "a million to one accident." Upon her return to England by ship, Markham wondered: "If I had known the Atlantic was as big as it seems, would I have had the courage to fly across?" Somehow, she doubted it.

The transatlantic flight proved to be an impossible act to follow for Beryl Markham. Never again would the aviator newspapers dubbed "The Beautiful Lady in Blue" capture the attention of the world in so startling and stunning a way. Though she went on to write a fascinating

"He wasn't a tall man," Beryl Markham wrote of her mentor Tom Campbell Black (1898-1936), *"but he had a quiet, convincing manner that made him look bigger than any job he ever held and more capable than any craft he ever flew."*

autobiography, *West with the Night*, and achieved international recognition when it was published in 1942, Markham's moment in the sun was behind her.

Hoping to break into the movies, Markham moved to California in 1939. After divorcing Mansfield in 1942, she married Raoul Schumacher, a writer who helped her with *West with the Night*. The couple enjoyed a lavish Hollywood social life, but the marriage eventually ended unhappily. In 1950, after her third divorce, Markham returned to the land she loved—Africa.

"Africa is never the same to anyone who leaves it and returns again," she wrote in *West with the Night*. "It is not a land of change, but it is a land of moods and its moods are numberless." When Markham left Africa in 1936, she had said, "I'll be back." Fourteen years later, she did come back, this time for good. She returned to horse racing and became one of Kenya's most successful trainers, winning the top trainer's award five times and the Kenya Derby six times. Amazingly enough, the woman who spent her thirties as a respected aviator seemed to have no regrets about giving up flying for the world of horse breeding and training. In an important way, by coming back to Africa and to horses, Markham was coming home, returning to the passion she and her father shared. Beryl Markham continued to train horses well into her eighties, and died in Kenya in 1986.

Beryl Markham in 1946

Anne Morrow Lindbergh (b. 1906) copiloted some of her famous husband's most daring flights, but she also gained recognition in her own right as a writer who introduced her readers to the beauty and excitement of flying.

5

Anne Morrow Lindbergh
Shy Pioneer

As Anne Morrow Lindbergh and her husband took off
from the waters off the west coast of Africa in their
Lockheed monoplane, Anne suddenly felt an overwhelm-
ing surge of empowerment. "Now, we are free," she
wrote. "We are up; we are off. We can toss you aside,
you there, way below us, a few lights in the great dark
silent world that is ours—for we are above it."

As a courageous aviator and the wife of the world-
famous Charles Lindbergh, Anne Morrow Lindbergh
helped pioneer commercial airline routes across the globe,

some of which are still in use today. Yet Anne was also a writer who captured her experiences in words, sharing with the world the beauty and freedom she found in the air.

Born on June 22, 1906, Anne Spencer Morrow was the second of four children in a privileged, well-educated family. Her father, Dwight Morrow, was a partner in the prestigious banking firm of J. P. Morgan & Company and later served the United States government in a variety of roles. Always on the go, Morrow rarely had time for his children, but he taught them a valuable maxim. "The world is divided into people who do things and people who get the credit," he said. "Try if you can to belong to the first class; there is far less competition."

Anne took her father's lesson to heart. In the fall of 1924, 18-year-old Anne entered her mother's alma mater, Smith College. There, she majored in creative writing and worked hard to develop her literary talent. "I want to write—I want to write—I want to write," she confided to her diary.

On the morning of May 20, 1927, while Anne was working on a paper in the college library, Charles Lindbergh, a 25-year-old airmail pilot, took off from a soggy runway on Long Island in the *Spirit of St. Louis*. Lindbergh hoped to win the $25,000 Orteig Prize, offered to the first pilot who flew from New York to Paris. This 3,500-mile journey would be the longest that had yet been accomplished in an airplane. Thirty-three hours later, Lindbergh successfully landed at Le Bourget airport just north of Paris, becoming the first person in the world to have flown the Atlantic solo. Americans went wild with pride, and Lindbergh became an immediate celebrity. Among the people fascinated by the aviation hero was Anne's father.

At the time, Dwight Morrow was employed by the United States government to study the importance of airplanes to national defense. After Lindbergh's historic flight, Morrow and President Calvin Coolidge realized that the young pilot would be a tremendous asset to the rapidly growing aviation industry. They invited him to Washington, D.C., to meet with them.

Six men had died attempting to fly across the Atlantic Ocean before Charles Augustus Lindbergh (1902-1974) made the flight successfully in 1927.

While Lindbergh was visiting the White House, President Coolidge asked the level-headed Morrow to become the ambassador to Mexico. Morrow accepted the post, despite the fact that relations between the United States and Mexico were strained. Coolidge's secretary of state considered Mexico's president, Plutarco Elías Calles, to be a communist. The American people were upset by the fact that the Mexican government had canceled American oil leases in Mexico and was threatening not to pay its foreign debts. To ease tensions, Morrow invited Lindbergh to make a publicity flight from Washington, D.C., to Mexico City in the *Spirit of St. Louis*. Not only would this be the first nonstop flight between the two cities, but Lindbergh's visit would also be a gesture of goodwill toward Mexico. The young pilot accepted, and his friendship with Morrow began.

After arriving in Mexico City on December 13, 1927, Charles stayed with the Morrow family at the American embassy. Anne, returning from college for her Christmas break, was introduced to him at an official reception in his honor. Shy, studious Anne doubted if she and America's hero would have anything in common, but that Christmas vacation changed everything. Back in the United States, Charles took Anne flying over Long Island and out for dinner and dancing in New York City. In December 1928, he asked Anne to become his wife.

After the wedding on May 27, 1929, Anne was suddenly forced to live her life in the public eye. The press followed the Lindberghs everywhere, and the couple was alone only in the sky.

But they both loved to fly. At first, Anne simply accompanied Charles on his flying adventures. Within two years of her marriage, however, with Charles as her exacting teacher, Anne became the first woman in the United States to earn a glider pilot's license, and then received her private pilot's license. She studied chart-making and navigation, learning to measure the angle of the sun and the position of the stars. She also became proficient in operating the high-frequency radio set, and eventually mastered the transmission and reception of Morse code. All this knowledge would be put to good use, for Anne was to become Charles's partner in flight. As her husband's copilot, she needed to be able to plot the plane's position, even in total darkness, and communicate with air traffic controllers.

Charles and Anne immediately began making major flights. In 1929, Anne flew an open-cockpit Curtiss Falcon biplane over the American southwest while Charles took hundreds of photographs in search of ancient cliff dwellings. That same year, the Lindberghs and three archaeologists flew to Central America to explore and photograph a Mayan ruin. In 1930, while Anne was seven months pregnant with their first son, she and Charles broke the transcontinental speed record by flying from Los Angeles to New York in 14 hours and 45 minutes, 3 hours faster than the previous record. The flight was strenuous for Anne, but she felt her participation could help prove the safety of air transportation.

The early 1930s marked the very beginning of the age of commercial air travel. Passenger airline services were just getting off the ground, and the Lindberghs contributed greatly to the growth of this industry. Together, they surveyed air routes for such newly emerging companies as Transcontinental and Western (TWA) and Pan American, testing weather and landing conditions to help airlines find the safest routes for passenger travel. On July 27, 1931, the Lindberghs took off on a survey trip to China via Canada, Alaska, Siberia, and Japan. Along the way, they would study the conditions encountered on an Arctic air route and track the time between destinations. Their goal was to chart a faster, more practical path to the Far East, proving that commercial flights were possible across far northern areas. This would prove to be their most historic mission.

The Lindberghs planned their route meticulously for this rigorous journey. Because they would be traveling over relatively unpopulated terrain, it was essential that their plan include precise points for refueling. The plane's gas tank also had to be large enough to accommodate long stretches of flying. At the same time, since gasoline is heavy, they had to calculate how to get by with as little fuel as possible. The Lindberghs' plane, *Sirius*, was fitted with special tanks that could hold enough gas for 2,000

Although the usual route to Asia was west across the Pacific Ocean, the Lindberghs took the shortest way by traveling north on what is called the Great Circle Route (shown above with some of their major stops).

miles of flying. Engineers also added pontoons instead of wheels, so that the plane could make water landings.

The Lindberghs had to be prepared for any situation. At the same time, everything they carried with them had to be essential because each pound made a difference in the air. In her book *North to the Orient*, which documents the trip, Anne recalled, "Every object taken had to be weighed, mentally as well as physically. The

Dressed in warm flight suits for their Arctic journey, Charles and Anne Lindbergh pose with their Lockheed airplane, Sirius.

weight in pounds must balance the value in usefulness. The floor of our room for weeks before our departure was covered with large untidy piles of equipment." The small plane needed to carry a 25-pound anchor, tools for repairs, a rubber boat, parachutes, firearms, a waterproof radio, a full medicine kit, food, fresh water, and warm clothes. Determined to have something nice to wear, Anne still brought along two pairs of shoes.

During the journey from the northwest territories of Canada to Alaska, the Lindberghs flew over rough and desolate territory. On August 4, they reached Point Barrow, Alaska, the northernmost point in their journey. They were supposed to refuel there, but discovered that the supply boat carrying their fuel had been stranded in the icy ocean 100 miles down the coast. With fuel running low, the Lindberghs had to fly on to Nome—about 600 miles away. Night began to fall when they were still an hour and a half from their destination. Unable to navigate around mountain peaks in the dark, Charles brought the plane down in the ocean. The couple had to spend the night in sleeping bags in the baggage compartment, and they reached Nome safely the following day.

At the end of August, the Lindberghs reached Asia. As the plane approached the island of Japan, Anne marveled at the landscape: "I looked down on the fairylike peaks, pushing their heads up through the mist," she wrote. "Every now and then we could see through a hole in the clouds a rocky beach or a strip of hare-bell-blue water gleam and vanish." Despite the beauty of the mountainous landscape, landing in Japan proved difficult. As the plane came in closer, the Lindberghs were surrounded by fog. They eventually brought the plane down in the water, and Anne found herself wondering, "What would the Japanese say to our landing?" The Japanese radio operator politely replied, "We—welcome—eagerly—you—here."

Crowds gathered to see Sirius *land off the coast of Japan. "I have never seen anything like the reception we got at Tokyo when we first arrived,"* Anne Lindbergh *wrote in a letter to her mother-in-law.*

In Tokyo, the Lindberghs met with the Japanese prime minister and the American ambassador. They also witnessed a traditional Japanese tea ceremony, which Anne found beautiful and deeply moving. After about two and a half weeks, they moved on to China, arriving in Nanking on September 19, 1931. There, they found that the 3,400-mile-long Yangtze River had flooded its banks, engulfing the lower Yangtze Valley in mud and water. Crops were destroyed and the livestock had drowned.

98

Millions of people had lost their homes and many were starving. At the time, *Sirius* was the only plane in China with sufficient range to survey the farthest reaches of the flood. Given the extreme circumstances, Charles and Anne quickly offered to stay on and help the National Flood Relief Commission.

Every day the Lindberghs flew out from Nanking. Sometimes, Anne piloted the airplane while Charles drew maps of the swollen river. When they flew doctors and medical supplies to flooded areas, Anne sat in the baggage compartment and looked out at the devastated landscape. "Flying lower," she wrote, "we could see suggestions of what the land was like under the flood: fields under water; hundreds of small villages standing in water, many of them up to their roofs; towns whose dykes and walls had given way, whose streets were canals." On one occasion, the Lindberghs narrowly escaped death when the crane lowering *Sirius* into the water jammed, tipping the plane over—with Charles and Anne in the cockpits. They had to jump clear of the plane, plunging into the rushing waters of the river.

While the plane was being repaired after this accident, Anne received word that her father had died. As soon as the Lindberghs heard the news, they canceled the rest of their survey flight and returned to America. Once they arrived home, their life on the ground became far more difficult than their grueling flight had been. The press had always hounded them tirelessly, and when

Anne Lindbergh holding her first son, Charles Augustus Jr. His birth (on Anne's twenty-fourth birthday, June 22, 1930) was international news, as was his tragic disappearance two years later.

tragedy struck, the Lindberghs' lack of privacy worsened. On March 1, 1932, their 20-month-old son, Charles, was kidnapped. For two and a half months, they negotiated with the kidnapper as the public stayed riveted to the case. Even though the Lindberghs paid the ransom money, they never saw their child alive again. On May 12, the small boy's dead body was found in the woods near their home.

Devastated, Anne did not return to flying until March 1933. Yet flying had always meant freedom for her. In the air, she and her husband were at their happiest, their lives "all gold." On July 9, 1933, they left on their most challenging adventure yet: a five-month series of study flights for Pan American Airways, testing air routes between the United States and Europe. The Lindberghs hoped to prove that a regular passenger service between the continents was feasible. Because early aviators were so vulnerable to the elements, many stretches of ocean had long been thought too dangerous to cross. The waters over which the Lindberghs would fly—particularly the turbulent North Atlantic—were the

Using their fame to publicize commercial airlines, Amelia Earhart (far left) and the Lindberghs (third and fourth from right) were passengers on a promotional flight for Transcontinental Air Transport.

last barriers to commercial air travel. To navigate these areas, the Lindberghs would need accurate maps and extensive statistics on weather, winds, and flying conditions. *Sirius* was fitted with a new and more powerful engine and renamed *Tingmissartoq*. In the Eskimo language, *Tingmissartoq* means "the one who flies like a big bird."

In total, the Lindberghs covered 30,000 miles, visiting 31 countries and colonies on 4 continents. Along the way, they braved blizzards, sandstorms, and even a hurricane. First, they flew from New York to Newfoundland, Canada, and crossed the Atlantic Ocean to Europe. The climate was most severe on this leg of the journey, especially over Greenland and Iceland. Then, between September and mid-November, the couple traveled down through Europe from Denmark to Portugal. Finally, they followed the Azores Route, which would eventually take them home.

This final flight involved flying down into Africa and along the equator to South America, before returning to New York via the Caribbean and Florida. Crossing the south Atlantic from Bathurst in Gambia to Natal in Brazil proved especially difficult. Loaded with enough fuel to fly 1,800 miles without stopping, the Lindberghs' plane was so heavy that it took three attempts on three different days to take off from the water off the coast of Gambia.

On the long flight across the Atlantic, Anne's endurance and her skill as a navigator were tested to their limits. At night, it was so dark in her cockpit that she had to become expert at operating the radio by touch alone.

Anne Lindbergh in her cockpit, which she called "my little room"

"Without sight, my fingers . . . knew the precise shape and spin of the small screws to open the radio boxes," she recalled. As the Lindberghs left the west coast of Africa, Anne proved her abilities dramatically. She made radio contact with a station on Long Island, New York, setting a world record of over 3,000 miles for communication between an airplane and a ground station.

Although the Lindberghs' five-month journey had been demanding and at times dangerous, it proved successful. Returning to the United States on December 16, the couple received a message of congratulation from President Franklin D. Roosevelt. Soon afterward, Anne became the first woman ever to receive the National

103

Geographic Society's Hubbard Medal. By proving that a regular passenger service between America and Europe was possible, she and Charles had helped shape the future of the aviation industry.

Anne felt a great sense of accomplishment, but she had not experienced the same exhilaration that she had felt on other flights. The truth was that after her son's death, Anne no longer felt invincible, and this trip had proved to be far more dangerous than any of the others.

In December 1935, the Lindberghs sailed for England with their three-year-old son, Jon. After suffering their first son's murder and the terrible strain of relentless publicity, the family no longer wanted to live in the United States. They spent four years in an English cottage, where a third son, Land, was born. Their two daughters, Anne and Reeve, and youngest son, Scott, were born during the years after they returned to the United States in 1939.

The Lindberghs continued to fly. They became interested in conservation in the 1960s, and in 1971, the couple built a house on the Hawaiian island of Maui, where they felt especially close to nature. On the morning of August 26, 1974, after 45 years of marriage, Charles Lindbergh died peacefully. Anne went on to write more books, published volumes of her diaries and letters, and in 1979 was inducted into the National Aviation Hall of Fame.

Because Anne Morrow Lindbergh was both an aviator and a writer, she made a great contribution to the

Anne Lindbergh pauses for reflection while attending the 1985 unveiling of a statue in St. Paul, Minnesota, commemorating her husband's achievements.

pioneering days of flight. Anne was able to capture in writing the visual and sensory beauty of flying during an era when air travel was brand new. "One could sit still and look at life from the air," she wrote. Anne once described her writings about aviation as "an attempt to capture some of the magic." The Lindberghs' extraordinary accomplishments gave Anne a lifetime of magical flying adventures to share in the pages of her books.

Jacqueline Cochran (1910?–1980) not only broke countless records in her career as an aviator, but also led the movement that brought women pilots into the United States military.

6

Jackie Cochran
At the Top of the World

*W*hen a plane travels faster than the speed of sound, listeners on the ground hear a noise like thunder. On May 18, 1953, at Edwards Air Force Base in California, Jacqueline Cochran made history with a thunderclap of her own. Cochran climbed to 45,000 feet in a Sabre jet. "Then," she later remembered, "I did a 'split S' to start the full-power and almost vertical dive and headed straight down for the airport as my target. I counted aloud the changing readings on the Mach meter. . . . Mach .97, Mach .98, Mach .99, Mach 1, Mach 1.01."

As she passed Mach 1, the speed of sound, Jackie Cochran became the first female pilot to break the sound barrier. But this was just one achievement in a supersonic rise to aviation fame. A woman considered alternately arrogant and an American hero, Jackie Cochran held more speed, altitude, and distance records than any other pilot, male or female, when she died in 1980.

A tough childhood in the Florida panhandle fueled Jackie Cochran's confidence and drive. When she was very young, she was either orphaned or abandoned by her birth parents. Because of this, no one was certain when she had been born, though it was probably between 1905 and 1910. Jackie never even knew her parents' names. According to a popular story, she chose the name "Cochran" for herself out of a phone book.

Adopted into a poor family living in a mill town in Florida, Jackie usually slept on the floor of the family home, a small shack with glassless windows and no plumbing. Jackie's foster father and brothers labored 14 hours a day in a sawmill and earned wooden tokens as payment. The company store, or commissary, was the only place that accepted these "chips" as money, and it charged high prices for food and household supplies. As a result, the family was always hungry and in debt to the store. "For the most part only dried beans and similar staples and meat such as bologna could be had in the commissary," Jackie recalled. "Oranges, even in that state of oranges, cost a nickel . . . and were above our means."

Jackie's foster father was a migrant worker, moving from town to town to find work. When Jackie was eight, the family moved to Georgia to work in a cotton mill, where raw cotton was transformed into thread, yarn, and fabric. Earning six cents an hour, Jackie worked 12-hour night shifts carrying yarn to weavers in the cotton mill. Within a year, she was supervising 15 other children at the factory.

When factory workers went on strike to protest cruel working conditions, Jackie found another job as live-in help for a family, cooking, cleaning, and baby-sitting. She soon started working in the beauty shop that the family owned. By the age of 15, she had learned the beautician's trade and was earning enough money to live on her own and buy a car.

She also saved enough money to attend nursing school for three years. At the end of the nursing course, Jackie worked as a nurse in a mill town similar to the one in which she was raised. One of her first jobs was delivering a baby for a family so poor that they had nothing to wrap the baby in when it was born. This experience prompted Jackie to return to beauty salon work. "I had neither the strength nor the money to do the smallest fraction of what had to be done for these people," she said, "and I determined that, if I was going to do anything for myself or others, I had to get away and make money."

Tired of living at the bottom of the heap, Jackie Cochran decided to start at the top. She moved north and talked her way into a job at a salon that was "all the rage" in New York—Antoine's of Saks Fifth Avenue. Antoine was impressed with her work and perseverance, and soon put her in charge of his salon in Miami Beach, Florida.

Despite her success, Cochran grew restless working in beauty salons and soon developed an idea for a business of her own: she would start a cosmetics company. With her determination and knowledge of the beauty field, she figured she could create the beauty products that women wanted. She continued to work at Antoine's, but nurtured her dream of her own business.

In 1932, Cochran met a man named Floyd Odlum in Miami. Cochran and Odlum connected easily because they were both ambitious and had similar histories. Odlum was a millionaire financier from New York, but he came from a humble background, like Cochran, and had built his fortune on his own by the time he was 36 years old.

Odlum listened to Cochran's idea of starting a cosmetics business. He commented that to sell enough of her products for her business to survive in the Great Depression, she "would almost need wings to cover the territory fast enough." Taking this remark literally, Cochran realized that having a pilot's license would give her a tremendous advantage as a businesswoman, helping her travel around the country to promote her company. She began taking flying lessons at Roosevelt Flying School on Long Island, paying $495 for 20 hours of instruction. In two and a half weeks, she earned her pilot's license.

Summarizing her rags-to-riches story and her love of flying, Jackie Cochran wrote, "I might have been born in a hovel but I determined to travel with the wind and the stars."

"When I paid for my first lesson, a beauty operator ceased to exist and an aviator was born," she later wrote.

Cochran had the flying bug. "There are so many wonderful things one can see while flying that earthbound souls miss," she said. Full of plans to make a career out of aviation, Cochran moved to San Diego and convinced a

Navy flight instructor to give her the equivalent of the U.S. Navy flight training. In a Travelair plane she bought for $1,200, she took more lessons and eventually earned her commercial license.

In 1935, with Floyd Odlum's help, Cochran founded Jacqueline Cochran Cosmetics. Within two years of launching her business, she opened a salon in Chicago and a cosmetics laboratory in New Jersey. Her aggressive business strategies brought her success, and she used her profits to finance her first love—flying.

It was lucky Cochran had another source of income, for although there were about 400 women pilots in the 1930s, nearly all the pilot jobs went to men. Cochran had to find another way to develop her flying career. She chose record-breaking and long-distance flying.

In 1934, Cochran entered the MacRobertson Race from England to Australia. Unfortunately, she was plagued by plane problems. On the way to start the race, her plane crashed in New Mexico. Cochran decided to borrow a Gee Bee racer, but this plane also malfunctioned and she was forced to drop out of the race.

Cochran fought hard to enter another race, the Bendix Cross-Country Air Race, a nonstop flight between Los Angeles and Cleveland. Only men were allowed to compete in this race until 1935, when she and Amelia Earhart entered the competition. Earhart captured fifth place, but Cochran was deeply disappointed when her plane malfunctioned near the Grand Canyon and she had to drop out of the race. Refusing to give up on the competition, Cochran entered again in 1937 and came in third. In the 1938 race, flying at an average airspeed of 250 miles per hour in a Seversky P-35, she placed first. She won the Bendix Trophy and a prize of $12,500.

Cochran also dedicated herself to setting as many records as she could. Between 1937 and 1940, she broke

After becoming the first woman to win the prestigious Bendix Trophy, Jackie Cochran is congratulated by Vincent Bendix (right), the race's founder, and Alexander de Seversky, the designer of her plane.

the women's national speed record, the women's world speed record, the New-York-to-Miami speed record, and an international speed record. In 1939, Cochran set a women's national altitude record as well, flying a small fabric-covered biplane to a height of 30,052 feet. At that height, the air is very thin and cold. Cochran ruptured a sinus blood vessel, got frostbite, and almost froze to death. Flying at such a high altitude made her dizzy and disoriented, and she had to fly at a lower altitude for an hour before she could think clearly enough to land the plane. This flight, along with her other achievements, landed Cochran soundly on the map of aviation fame.

Cochran's personal life was also soaring. On May 10, 1936, she married her long-time friend and love Floyd Odlum. Their marriage lasted 40 years, during which they lived in many different parts of the country. Their favorite place was their ranch in southern California.

Amelia Earhart, who had been a close friend of Cochran's since they competed in the 1935 Bendix Race, often spent time at the ranch with her husband, George Putnam. On June 1, 1937, Cochran and Odlum went to the Miami airport to see Earhart off on her flight around the world. Although Cochran had a bad feeling about Earhart's groundbreaking venture, she didn't realize she would never see her friend again. She was devastated when Earhart disappeared, but even more determined to succeed as an aviator. In a speech in Earhart's honor, Cochran said that Earhart "had merely placed the torch in the hands of others to carry on to the next goal, and from there on and on forever."

While war was brewing in Europe, Cochran worked for airplane manufacturers testing new features in warplanes. Once World War II began in 1939, the United States supported its allies, Great Britain and France, by providing airplanes and supplies. By 1940, the United States was mobilizing for possible involvement in the war, and men began to be drafted into the military. Cochran saw a tremendous opportunity for women pilots to contribute to the preparations for war: they could take over transporting planes from the United States to Europe, leaving more men free for combat if necessary. Cochran hurried to seize the chance. On June 17, 1941, she became the first woman to ferry a bomber across the North Atlantic, flying a Lockheed Hudson from Canada to Scotland. Although her achievement did not convince the American government to employ women pilots, Cochran was asked to organize and train a group of 25 American women to ferry planes for the British government.

On December 7, 1941, the Japanese bombed Pearl Harbor, Hawaii, and shortly afterward the United States declared war on Japan and its allies, Germany and Italy. Once the United States was involved in the war, military leaders soon faced a shortage of manpower to fuel the war effort. Thus, in 1943, Cochran's long struggle to convince the American government that women pilots could be useful finally succeeded. General Henry "Hap"

Jackie Cochran discusses her plans to organize women ferry pilots in England with Captain Norman Edgar, a representative of the British Transport Auxiliary.

Arnold asked her to return from England to train female pilots for the U.S. Army Air Force in a program that became known as the Women's Air Force Service Pilots (WASP).

As director of the WASP, Cochran was to supervise and coordinate training for women pilots who would be assigned to the Air Transport Command (ATC). The

ATC was in charge of ferrying new fighter and bomber planes to air bases within the United States. Cochran chose 28 women for the first class of training and set up the program in record time. This first group of pilots trained for 30 to 40 days, learning airplane maintenance, navigation, meteorology, math skills, military law, and flying. By the end of the war, over 25,000 women had applied for the program and 1,074 graduated from training.

Jackie Cochran instructs a group of WASPs at Camp Davis Army Air Field in North Carolina.

117

As the Army gained confidence in the WASP program, female pilots took on a variety of important tasks. In addition to ferrying all kinds of military aircraft throughout the United States for the ATC, they participated in target practice for the Army Air Force. WASPs flew planes with streamers attached to the tails, while gunners on the ground and combat pilots in the air practiced their aim by shooting at the streamers. Since WASPs were always in danger of being shot down by accident, flying planes for target practice was a dangerous job. It played a central role, however, in evaluating the combat skills of gunners and pilots. WASPs also served as test pilots, flying newly repaired planes to help mechanics determine whether problems had been successfully corrected. Test flying was so hazardous that many male pilots preferred to risk their lives in combat, and WASPs took over almost all the test flying missions at some air bases.

At first, there was no WASP uniform, and the pilots did their work in men's flight suits that were far too big for them. From her days as a beautician, Cochran was always interested in helping people look their best, and she used her own money to have uniforms for the WASP designed at a fancy New York department store, Bergdorf Goodman. Cochran wanted the WASPs to be as professional, respectable, and distinguished as the Army Air Force pilots.

Indeed, Cochran firmly believed that the WASPs were equal to their male counterparts in every way.

WASPs Eloise Huffines, Millie Davidson, Elizabeth MacKethan, and Clara Jo Marsh in their uniforms

During the war, women pilots flew approximately 60 million miles for the Army Air Force, with lower accident and death rates than those for male pilots in similar work. In her final report to General Arnold, Cochran pointed out that the WASP program demonstrated that "women . . . could be trained as quickly and as economically as men in the same age group to fly all types of planes safely, efficiently, and regularly, . . . that women pilots have as much stamina and endurance and are no more subject to operational or flying fatigue than male pilots doing similar work and can fly as many hours per month as male pilots; and that an effective women's air force of many scores of thousands of good dependable pilots could be built up in case of need."

Cochran wanted the Women's Air Force Service Pilots to be recognized as enlisted members of the U.S. military. A bill to militarize the WASP was sent to Congress, but it was defeated in the Senate because the war was almost over and few people believed there would be a need for female military pilots in the future. This defeat bitterly disappointed Cochran. It was not until 1977 that the WASP was recognized as part of the Army and its members finally received veteran's benefits for their wartime service.

After the war, manufacturers began developing jet airplanes. As Cochran said, "Since I had started flying in 1932 until the jet phase came along, I had been in the center of aviation. But the jet phase was threatening to pass me by." This was because only United States Air Force pilots were allowed to fly jet planes, and women were not allowed to fly for the military. With her trademark determination, Cochran struggled for two years to gain access to a jet. Finally, she got around the American military policy by learning to fly a Canadian-owned plane, the Sabre jet.

Jackie Cochran listens to tips on supersonic jet flying from the famous aviator Chuck Yeager (left).

121

Cochran began going after speed records in the jet, but she longed for more new frontiers of aviation. In 1953, General Chuck Yeager, a friend of Cochran's and the first person to break the sound barrier, began helping her learn how to make a supersonic flight. On May 18, Cochran became the first woman to exceed the speed of sound. Two weeks later, before an audience of journalists and photographers, she and Yeager climbed to 50,000 feet in two separate jets. They dove earthward simultaneously, breaking the sound barrier again in what Cochran called "a sort of supersonic duet."

By June 1953, Cochran held all but one of the major world speed records for straight-line and closed-course flight. Despite increasing health problems, she continued to break records into her 50s and 60s. In 1962, she became the first woman to fly a jet across the Atlantic. That same year, she set 69 intercity and straight-line distance records and 9 international speed, distance, and altitude records. Within several years of these achievements, however, kidney problems and a weakened heart grounded Cochran permanently. She and Odlum continued to spend time together at their California ranch until his death in 1976. Her health began to decline further, and in 1980, Jacqueline Cochran died.

Cochran received countless distinctions and honors during her career, including being elected president of the Fédération Aéronautique Internationale and becoming the first woman to be enshrined in the Aviation Hall

Jackie Cochran being interviewed after her record-setting flight from New Orleans to Bonn, Germany, in 1968. At her side is her husband, Floyd Odlum.

of Fame. In addition to convincing the military to use and recognize the service of women pilots, she encouraged women to take part in aviation and space programs. Raised in an impoverished mill town, she knew and worked with presidents Franklin Roosevelt, Harry Truman, and Dwight Eisenhower. As Chuck Yeager wrote, "Sometimes even Jackie Cochran couldn't believe what she had accomplished."

Cochran's own words describing her career were simple: "Adventure is a state of mind—and spirit. It comes with faith, for with complete faith there is no fear of what faces you in life or death. In truth, I ended up living a life of continuous adventure."

Patricia Bowser and Ann Waldner, members of the Women's Air Force Service Pilots (WASP), fly a B-17 Flying Fortress during World War II. The WASP program paved the way for women in military aviation today.

7

Modern Women in Aviation

*A*t the end of World War II, the future of women in aviation seemed to be in jeopardy. An unprecedented number of women had been recruited to aviation-related jobs during the war, but high levels of aircraft production and military personnel were unnecessary in peacetime. After the upheaval of the war years, most people wanted society to return to its "normal" state—which included keeping women in their traditional roles. But progress had been made, and it could not be so easily reversed. Despite the fact that many of them lost their wartime jobs, the number of women working in the aircraft industry remained higher than before the war and only continued to rise in the following decades. The question was gradually becoming *how*, not *whether*, women would participate in the field of aviation.

The military wanted to be able to mobilize quickly in case of another war, and this involved keeping women trained to take over non-combat jobs. Thus, in 1948, Congress passed the Women's Armed Services Act to establish women's reserves in all branches of the peacetime military. Unfortunately, the real motive behind the act was to make women available as secretaries and other support staff. These roles had become essential to the military during World War II, but were considered less suitable for men. In the Korean War in the 1950s, however, military women were briefly able to use their abilities as flight instructors, mechanics, and air traffic controllers.

In the 1960s, opportunities for women in military aviation sank to a new low. Out of 61 non-combat jobs, only 36 were open to women—70 percent in clerical work and 23 percent in medicine. But with the escalation of the Vietnam War toward the end of the decade, the military found that not only did it need women to take over non-combat duties while men went to war, but it was also facing a severe shortage of new recruits. Because some Americans believed the war to be unjust, they were unwilling to volunteer for armed service. But thousands of women were clamoring to join the armed forces and were being turned away because of limits on the number of women in the military. Even after beginning to draft men in 1967, the military realized it would be wise to accept anyone who was willing to serve. That year, a new law was passed removing all restrictions on the number of women in the armed forces and allowing female officers to be promoted to high ranks that previously had been closed to them.

The equal rights movement in the late 1960s and early 1970s made some military leaders worry that they

The first enlisted women in the Air Force to be assigned to Vietnam arrived at Tan Son Nhut Air Base in June 1967.

would soon be required by law to allow women to participate in more military occupations. They began to recruit women more heavily, examining new ways to employ them. Finally, 30 years after the WASPs flew during World War II, women began to be trained as military pilots. In 1974, the Navy chose its first six noncombatant female pilots and Lieutenant Sally Murphy became the first female U.S. Army pilot. Two years later, the Air Force followed suit and began to train women.

As women became more fully involved, significant changes were necessary in many aspects of military life. For example, aircraft designers had always built airplane cockpits to fit men's bodies. Now, for safety as well as comfort, military aircraft had to be reconfigured to take into account a woman's average height, sitting position, reach, and eye level. To include women permanently in the armed forces, officials had to rethink everything from facilities to uniform design. To male members of the military, it seemed that women were upsetting the system.

Linda Hutton understood the resentment and discrimination she encountered after becoming the seventh woman to earn her wings as a U.S. Navy pilot. "I felt it was perfectly within their rights," she said. "I mean, here I was breaking into their domain." Hutton decided she could succeed while ignoring the rude comments and hostile attitudes of some of her peers. After all, she had work to do. "When I first came in the Navy [in 1975] and received my wings," she recalled, "women could not land on any kind of ship in any kind of airplane. Then the Navy opened up helicopters, letting women land on ships. The first woman landed on an aircraft carrier in '79, and it's been step-by-step ever since."

By 1996, Hutton had logged over 385 aircraft landings on carrier ships, a job requiring precision maneuvering. That year, she became the first woman to command a naval air station when she was promoted to captain of Major Naval Command in Key West, Florida. Hutton found satisfaction not only in the success, excitement, and challenge of her work, but also in working with people in the Navy from all over the United States. "They each come with their own agenda, their own goals and aspirations," she said. "And the opportunity to work with them is an opportunity to work not just *for* your country but *with* your country."

While Hutton struggled to prove her merit to her male peers, Krista Bonino, 19 years younger, could confidently say, "To me it's no big deal. . . . My role is the same as any other pilot's role. Whatever mission is handed down, nothing is changed because of gender." When she spoke these words in 1996, Bonino was a 26-year-old first lieutenant piloting an OH-58D Kiowa Warrior helicopter in the U.S. Army. The casualness with which she referred to her work shows how far women have come since Harriet Quimby donned a male disguise in order to learn to fly. Although military women saw action in the Persian Gulf War in 1991, it was not until 1993 that the Secretary

Three female pilots of the Navy's Tactical Electronic Warfare Squadron 34 posing in front of an F/A-18A Hornet aircraft in 1992

of Defense established a new assignment rule that allowed women to serve in combat aircraft and ships. By 1994, 92 percent of all career fields in the military were open to women, although female members of the armed forces are still excluded from direct ground combat. Today, women make up 14 percent of the armed forces, leaving room for future pioneers to enter this challenging arena.

Women's achievements in other areas of aviation have paralleled their fight for acceptance in the military. It was not until 1973, for instance, that Emily Warner became the first female commercial airline pilot. For years, she had trained male students and watched them find jobs with commercial airlines long before Frontier Airlines finally hired her. When asked why Warner had been hired, an airline spokesperson said, "We couldn't think of any reason not to." Since then, over 4,000 women have followed in Warner's footsteps, although they still constitute only 3 percent of all airline pilots.

Continuing the tradition of the barnstormers of the 1920s, women have also made advances as aerobatic pilots. It is estimated that aerobatics is the second largest spectator sport in the United States, surpassed only by baseball. For audiences, stunt flying is colorful and thrilling; for pilots, it demands daring, physical and mental discipline, and countless hours of practice. "When you first start doing it, you feel like your head's going to explode and your eyeballs are going to pop out," Patty Wagstaff has said of flying upside down and other aerobatic stunts. One of the best-known and most successful aerobatic pilots, Wagstaff was a six-time member of the U.S. aerobatic team and became the first woman ever to win the National Aerobatic Championship. Despite the stress of competition and the danger of her daredevil stunts, Wagstaff continues to thrive in the air, calling it "my element."

Patty Wagstaff is one of the few pilots in the world to make a career in both competition aerobatics and professional air show flying.

Before taking flight, this adventurous and free-spirited woman lived in California, Japan, Switzerland, England, and Alaska while working a number of odd jobs as a waitress, chauffeur, model, factory worker, and office manager. It was in Alaska in 1979 that Patty met Bob Wagstaff, an attorney and flight instructor whom she later married. He began giving her flight lessons, and on September 10, 1980, she earned her private pilot's license. In 1982, she began to study aerobatics with instructor Darlene Dubay. To Patty, these lessons were "my first heady sip of what would become an intoxication. My wild side took to aerobatics like one who had been kept in darkness and was suddenly led into blinding light."

In 1984, Patty Wagstaff bought her first aerobatic plane, began to perform in air shows, and soon entered her first aerobatic contest. Making up for her lack of experience with enthusiasm and determination, she quickly jumped into the highest possible level of competition. There was one available spot on the women's U.S. aerobatic team, and Wagstaff intended to win it. To do so, she had to compete against five other women in the most advanced category at the 1985 National Aerobatic Championship.

For this contest, Wagstaff performed three flights. The first, the compulsory, tested specific skills, while the second, the freestyle, she choreographed herself. The third flight, the unknown, was the most challenging. Wagstaff was given a list of maneuvers to learn for this event, but was not told the sequence in which she must perform them until just 24 hours before she took to the air. She was not allowed to practice the sequence at all, so learning it was a strenuous mental exercise. Under one of the major rules of aerobatic competition, Wagstaff was required to perform all three of her routines within a space in the air 3,300 feet wide and 3,300 feet tall; she could be penalized for flying outside of this "aerobatic box." She was judged on the precision, balance, and style with which she executed her maneuvers.

In 1985, her first year of national competition, Wagstaff attained her goal of qualifying for the U.S. aerobatic team, which competes every two years at the World Aerobatic Championship. Although Wagstaff won a place on the national team five more consecutive times, she had already set her sights on an even greater achievement: winning the National Aerobatic Championship. In 1991, she became the first—and, so far, the only—woman to win, and went on to take first place again in 1992 and 1993. Wagstaff also made a name for herself as an air show performer and launched her own business, Patty Wagstaff Airshows, to manage and publicize her career. In March 1994, as a recognition of her many accomplishments, Wagstaff's Extra 260 airplane was placed in the National Air and Space Museum in Washington, D.C. It now stands alongside Amelia Earhart's Lockheed Vega and Charles and Anne Lindbergh's Lockheed Sirius in the Pioneers of Flight exhibit.

What was Wagstaff's secret of success? Mental preparation was one key. She began visualizing her stunts months in advance of any competition. In bed at night, she went through the routines in her mind until she fell asleep. Then, when the time came, she was focused and ready. In truth, Wagstaff never minded the stress of competition. "I knew from the first time I saw aerobatics performed that it would take a lot of practice," she said, "but it was a mountain that I'd wanted to climb, a challenge that loomed larger than life. This was what I'd

Patty Wagstaff performs a flight stunt

been waiting for—something big to commit to, something exciting into which to throw my energies."

Although there are still separate categories for men and women at the international level, in the United States they have competed equally in aerobatic competitions since 1972. Yet Wagstaff's experience has proven that some people still consider aerobatics a male domain. As she began to present a serious challenge to men in competitions, she heard comments like, "Watch out for that little airplane, honey!" or "Hey, babe, d'ya know what you're doin'?" While Wagstaff always wondered, "Would you say that to one of the guys?" the sexism she encountered only increased her ambition. "I had to *show* people that I could be serious, capable, and dedicated," she wrote in her autobiography. "I realized that in order to change perceptions of women in aviation, women in aerobatics, I had to initiate an education process—my own and that of others. This actually served to cement my goal to be the best pilot, not just the best woman pilot. I knew I could do anything in an airplane as well or better than anyone else and I hoped that the time would come that I could be judged as a pilot, not as a woman pilot."

With similar goals, women also continue to break flying records. Twenty-two years after Geraldine Mack became the first woman to fly around the world, Jeana Yeager copiloted the first ever nonstop, unrefueled around-the-world flight. "Growing up," Yeager said, "I learned that I could do anything I set my mind to if I was willing to work hard enough." She brought this determination and confidence to flying, and spent years preparing for the historic 1986 flight that would test her skill and endurance to the limit.

Yeager had always been an ambitious, adventurous, and active person. She ran track during high school and spent as much time as possible around the horses her father bred. First attracted to aviation because of a child-hood fascination with helicopters and the freedom they seemed to represent, Yeager eventually learned to fly in Santa Rosa, California, and earned her license in 1978 at the age of 26. Since she liked to draw, Yeager also learned drafting (drawing plans for engineers). Her growing interest in aeronautic engineering eventually led her to the Rutan Aircraft Company in Mojave, California, where she befriended two brothers—Dick and Burt Rutan.

When Yeager met them in 1980, Dick, a former jet fighter pilot, was working for his younger brother Burt, a designer and builder of small, efficient airplanes. Together, the three of them hatched a plan to create a plane that could fly around the world. The project—which Yeager named, appropriately, *Voyager*—became their shared passion for the next six years.

The plane that Jeana Yeager and Dick Rutan would fly around the world was built using the most innovative design technology. Burt Rutan had calculated that to carry the enormous load of fuel required to fly all the way around the world—7,000 pounds, to be exact—a traditional aluminum airplane would need to be the size of an aircraft carrier. Instead, he designed a composite structure (a structure made of layers of different materials) for *Voyager*. Using a plastic-coated paper honeycomb sandwiched between two layers of graphite-fiber tape, Burt created an extremely strong structure that weighed only 939 pounds, less than a compact car. Because the materials were not chemically affected by fuel, the body of the airplane itself could be used to store fuel. The inside spaces of the the wings and even part of the fuselage (the body of the plane) became 17 distinct fuel tanks that held a total of almost 1,500 gallons, as much as a tanker truck.

Even though they had decided to build *Voyager* themselves, Jeana, Dick, and Burt still had to raise the hundreds of thousands of dollars they would need to make their plans a reality. They set up a corporation, Voyager Aircraft, and invested all their money in it. Then they assembled a team of workers, many of them volunteers who were excited by the idea of the project. Jeana and Dick wrote proposals for potential sponsors, made speeches, gave endorsements, and even sold souvenir hats and T-shirts. They lived on a tight budget, putting every cent they earned into building *Voyager*.

In 1981, Jeana and Dick began breaking records in another of Burt's planes, the Long EZ, to attract publicity and gain flying experience. During a cross-country race, Jeana faced a sudden emergency when one of the plane's propeller blades broke off. There was only one open space in which to land: the middle of the interstate highway! Without hesitating, Jeana brought the plane down between some big trucks and an overpass bridge. Skidding under the overpass, she moved the plane right along with the cars going in the same direction. Then she simply jumped out and pushed the plane to the side of the road so she wouldn't hold up traffic. Jeana's ability to remain cool and collected in high-pressure situations convinced Dick that "Jeana possessed her own special brand of courage."

Voyager was finally finished and ready for test flights in 1984. On their first flight together, Jeana and Dick discovered that despite Burt's efforts to make the plane as

Jeana Yeager works on Voyager. *The aircraft is shaped like a large, open square with the main body of the plane in the center and long wings extending outward on either side.*

stable as possible, its light and flexible construction led to one dangerous quirk. When the plane encountered even mild turbulence, the long wings began to flap several feet up and down. The plane would "porpoise" through the air, its nose rising and falling despite the pilot's efforts. Dick was exhausted by trying to control the airplane, but Jeana bore the worst of the turbulence. As copilot, she had to be able to move around the cabin and could not be strapped in as Dick was. Later, she recalled being airsick for the first time in her life as she "bounced all around the cockpit, spent half the time on the ceiling, and came out bruised and battered." It was too late to redesign *Voyager*, however. To avoid the deadly porpoising, Jeana and Dick chose a flight route that would keep them out of stormy areas. Then, for the next two years, they flew the plane with increasing levels of fuel in the tanks to determine how it would handle when it was heavily loaded.

In July 1986, Jeana Yeager and Dick Rutan made an impressive flight that attracted a great deal of publicity and donations for *Voyager*. Flying up and down the California coast for four days, they broke the world record for a closed-course unrefueled flight and set three other distance and endurance records. They had flown a total of 11,857 miles, about half the distance around the globe.

This accomplishment proved that *Voyager* was ready, and on December 13, 1986, the plane was flown to the point of departure—Edwards Air Force Base near Mojave, California. Edwards has one of the longest runways in the

140

world, and the gasoline-heavy plane needed all 15,000 feet of it to get off the ground. When *Voyager* took off at 8:00 A.M. on December 14, its tanks were so full that the tips of its wings scraped the ground.

By the first evening of the flight, *Voyager* was headed west over the Pacific, just south of Hawaii. The plane had been designed with two engines in tandem, one at the front end of the fuselage and the other at the rear. This allowed the pilots to turn off one engine to conserve fuel without throwing the plane off balance. At the beginning of the flight, however, the plane was too heavy to rely on just one engine. Until the fourth day, Yeager and Rutan were forced to use both of the plane's engines, burning more fuel than they had planned.

Rutan was to fly the majority of the journey, while Yeager was responsible for navigation, checking the instruments, pumping gasoline from one tank to another to keep the plane balanced, operating the landing gear, and recording everything in the airplane log book. After more than 55 hours in the pilot's seat, Rutan was exhausted and Yeager took over, flying *Voyager* over the Philippines and the South China Sea.

How did the pilots change places in a cockpit only three and a half feet wide and seven and a half feet long? *Voyager*'s pilot's seat was on the right side of the fuselage, while the copilot lay on a narrow cushioned bunk along-side and behind the pilot. This way, the pilot and copilot were able to take turns flying and lying down to rest and sleep. To change places, Rutan had to slide sideways off the seat. Then Yeager squeezed her legs up and onto the seat behind him, wriggling up into the pilot's seat. Meanwhile, Rutan pulled himself back onto the bunk. The change of places took about a minute, but proved almost impossible in rough weather.

The demanding nature of flying *Voyager* left little time for anything else. Both pilots found it difficult to sleep, and averaged only about two hours of rest per night. They had taken only the simplest foods along, packed in plastic pouches that were irradiated to kill bacteria and prevent spoilage. Mostly, Yeager and Rutan ate dried, ready-to-eat food, like Shaklee peanut butter crunch energy bars (their favorite snack), cereals, crackers, and fruits. In addition, they had 90 pounds of water in collapsible plastic containers and a hot-water heater for preparing warm drinks and instant soup. Yet they were so busy with the flight that they wound up eating only one-third of the food they brought. As for the disposal of human waste, it was primitive at best. For urinating, they used a relief tube, a plastic funnel with a tube leading outside the cabin. For solid waste, they used plastic containment bags which they dropped overboard through a little door in the bottom of the plane or stored with other refuse in a special compartment.

On December 18, halfway between India and the coast of Africa, *Voyager* broke the record for the world's longest unrefueled flight. Then, over the mountains of

142

west central Africa, the plane encountered bad weather and heavy turbulence. Rutan had to fly up to an altitude of 20,000 feet to find smoother air, and both pilots wore oxygen equipment to keep their minds clear. Still, fatigue began to paralyze Rutan. Feeling as if he were floating in a fog, he began to hallucinate that the instrument panel was bulging. He could not concentrate on flying, and Yeager spent a long time convincing him that it was necessary for them to change places. "I had to talk him back into the rest area," she said later. "He kept babbling about the panel and trying to push it back into place. I knew he was in trouble. . . . I was in bad shape, but Dick was worse."

Throughout the flight, the pilots had worried about the amount of fuel because they knew that every drop was important. But by the time they reached the final stretch of their flight—over the Atlantic, across Central America, and up the Pacific coast to California—no one was really certain how much fuel *Voyager* had left. Four hundred and fifty miles from home, the plane's rear engine stopped. As Rutan desperately tried to start the front engine, the plane dropped over 3,000 feet in altitude. Both engines finally started, but the pilots and ground crew suspected that the rear engine had failed because the fuel tanks it drew from were empty. Later, Yeager and Rutan discovered that they had had only five usable gallons of fuel left when they landed at Edwards Air Force Base on December 23.

Jeana Yeager and Dick Rutan receive a certificate of record from the National Aeronautic Association for the first nonstop unrefueled around-the-world flight.

About 30,000 people turned out to watch *Voyager* arrive at Edwards and millions more were watching on live television. Jeana Yeager and Dick Rutan had been in the air for 9 days, 3 minutes, and 44 seconds, flying a total of 24,986 miles. After they had a chance to recover, Jeana, Dick, and Burt were presented with the Presidential Citizens Award by President Ronald Reagan on December 29. They also received the Collier Trophy, aviation's most prestigious honor.

The example of Jeana Yeager and her unparalleled around-the-world flight is evidence of how far women pilots have come since the early days of Harriet Quimby and Amelia Earhart. Throughout the *Voyager* flight, Yeager received little special attention as a woman. "She just likes to get on with the job," commented Mission Control at Edwards Air Force Base, "and she is very much an equal partner in this."

Women pilots who break records, along with women who fly in the military, in the commercial airline industry, and in the heady, often dangerous field of aerobatic competition, have had to work hard to prove their abilities just because they are women. Although these women did not play a role in the early years of aviation, they are still pioneers. With their success, they are helping to ensure that future women will find equality in the air. A sign of optimism may be that in 2000, 11.5 percent of student pilots were female. Despite the fact that only 6 percent of active certified pilots were women, nearly double that number were determined to learn to fly. Jeana Yeager called *Voyager*'s flight "the last first in aviation," but given aviation's vibrant history during the past century and the progress still to be made, it seems likely that there are many more "firsts" ahead.

Glossary of Aviation Terms

aerial: relating to flight or aircraft

aerobatics: maneuvers carried out by an aircraft's pilot that are not necessary for normal flight, such as stunt flying

aerodrome: a French word for airport or airfield, a place for the takeoff and landing of aircraft

aeronautic: dealing with flight within the Earth's atmosphere

airstrip: a natural surface adapted for the operation of aircraft

altimeter: an aircraft instrument used for determining altitude

altitude: the height of an object above a given level, such as feet above sea level

aviator: the pilot of a glider, airplane, or helicopter

aviatrix: a female pilot. The word is rarely used today, since most people prefer the gender-neutral term "aviator."

barnstorming: traveling from place to place to participate in air shows as a pilot or other performer

barrel roll: a flight maneuver in which an aircraft makes a complete horizontal rotation while maintaining its original direction

biplane: an airplane with two sets of main wings, one above the other

cabin: an enclosed compartment for the passengers of an aircraft

cockpit: the compartment, generally at the front of the cabin, from which the pilot and crew control an aircraft

composite: an aircraft made of layers of different materials

figure eight: a flight maneuver that follows the shape of a numeral 8

fuselage: the body of an aircraft

glider: an unpowered aircraft used for gliding or soaring

headwind: a wind blowing directly against the course of an aircraft

horsepower: a unit of power equal to 745.7 watts

jet: an aircraft powered by a jet engine, in which air and fuel are burned together in a combustion chamber. The resulting jet of exhaust drives the aircraft forward.

loop-the-loop: a flight maneuver in which an aircraft makes a complete vertical circle

Mach number: the ratio of an aircraft's speed to the speed of sound. Mach 1 is the speed of sound, or 760 mph at sea level (it decreases with greater altitude), Mach 2 is twice the speed of sound, and so forth.

meteorology: the science that deals with phenomena of the atmosphere, especially weather

monoplane: an airplane with one set of wings

pontoon: the float on a seaplane

radar: a method of navigation that uses radio waves to find location and direction of objects

runway: a strip of level, usually paved, ground from which aircraft can take off and land

seaplane: an aircraft that takes off from and lands in water

supersonic: travel at speeds exceeding the speed of sound

throttle: the lever or pedal controlling the flow of fuel in an engine, and thus the speed of an aircraft

turbulence: violent, "bumpy" movement of an aircraft caused by disturbances in the atmosphere

Bibliography

Boase, Wendy. *The Sky's the Limit: Women Pioneers in Aviation*. New York: Macmillan, 1979.

Brooks-Pazmany, Kathleen. *United States Women in Aviation 1919-1929*. Washington, D.C.: Smithsonian Institution Press, 1983.

Butler, Susan. *East to the Dawn: The Life of Amelia Earhart*. Reading, Mass.: Addison-Wesley, 1997.

Cochran, Jacqueline. *The Stars at Noon*. Boston: Little, Brown, 1954.

Douglas, Deborah G. *United States Women in Aviation 1940-1985*. Washington, D.C.: Smithsonian Institution Press, 1990.

Earhart, Amelia. *Last Flight*. New York: Orion, 1988.

Federal Aviation Administration. "Airmen Certification FAQ." registry.faa.gov/faqam.htm, cited February 22, 2000.

Hall, Ed Y. *Harriet Quimby: America's First Lady of the Air*. Spartanburg, N.C.: Honoribus, 1990.

Harriet Quimby Research Conference. "Harriet Quimby's Flight Across the English Channel, 1912." www.harrietquimby.org, cited August 11, 2000.

Haynesworth, Leslie and David Toomey. *Amelia Earhart's Daughters: The Wild and Glorious Story of American Women Aviators from World War II to the Dawn of the Space Age*. New York: William Morrow, 1998.

Herrmann, Dorothy. *Anne Morrow Lindbergh: A Gift for Life*. New York: Ticknor & Fields, 1993.

Holden, Henry M. *Her Mentor Was an Albatross: The Autobiography of Pioneer Pilot Harriet Quimby*. Mt. Freedom, N.J.: Black Hawk, 1993.

Holden, Henry M. and Captain Lori Griffith. *Ladybirds II: The Continuing Story of American Women in Aviation*. Mt. Freedom, N.J.: Black Hawk, 1993.

Jones, Terry Gwynn. "For a Brief Moment the World Seemed Wild About Harriet." *Smithsonian*, January 1984.

Kaufmann, John. *Voyager: Flight Around the World*. Hillside, N.J.: Enslow, 1989.

Lindbergh, Anne Morrow. *Bring Me a Unicorn: Diaries and Letters of Anne Morrow Lindbergh 1922-1928*. New York: Harcourt Brace, 1971.

———. *Hour of Gold, Hour of Lead: Diaries and Letters of Anne Morrow Lindbergh 1929-1932*. New York: Harcourt Brace, 1973.

———. *Listen! the Wind*. New York: Harcourt Brace, 1938.

———. *Locked Rooms and Open Doors: Diaries and Letters of Anne Morrow Lindbergh 1933-1935*. New York: Harcourt Brace, 1974.

———. *North to the Orient*. New York: Harcourt Brace, 1967.

Lomax, Judy. *Women of the Air*. New York: Ivy Books, 1986.

Lovell, Mary S. *The Sound of Wings: The Life of Amelia Earhart*. New York: St. Martin's, 1989.

150

————. *Straight on Till Morning: The Biography of Beryl Markham*. New York: St. Martin's, 1987.

Markham, Beryl. *West with the Night*. San Francisco: North Point Press, 1983.

Milton, Joyce. *Loss of Eden: A Biography of Charles and Anne Morrow Lindbergh*. New York: HarperCollins, 1993.

Motor Sports Hall of Fame. "Jacqueline Cochran." www.mshf.com/hof/cochran.htm, cited September 16, 1999.

Oakes, Claudia M. *United States Women in Aviation through World War I*. Washington, D.C.: Smithsonian Institution Press, 1978.

————. *United States Women in Aviation 1930-1939*. Washington, D.C.: Smithsonian Institution Press, 1991.

Randolph, Blythe. *Amelia Earhart*. New York: Franklin Watts, 1987.

Rich, Doris L. *Amelia Earhart: A Biography*. Washington, D.C.: Smithsonian Institution Press, 1989.

————. *Queen Bess: Daredevil Aviator*. Washington, D.C.: Smithsonian Institution Press, 1993.

Russo, Carolyn. *Women and Flight: Portraits of Contemporary Women Pilots*. Boston: Bullfinch, 1997.

Taylor, Richard L. *The First Unrefueled Flight Around the World: The Story of Dick Rutan and Jeana Yeager and Their Airplane, Voyager*. New York: Franklin Watts, 1994.

Trzebinski, Errol. *The Lives of Beryl Markham*. New York: W.W. Norton, 1993.

United States Department of Defense. "Assignment Policy for Women in the Military." dticaw.dtic.mil/prhome/assignpo.html, cited February 22, 2000.

Van Wagenen Kiel, Sally. *Those Wonderful Women in Their Flying Machines: The Unknown Heroines of World War II*. New York: Rawson, Wade, 1979.

Wagstaff, Patty with Ann L. Cooper. *Fire and Air: A Life on the Edge*. Chicago: Chicago Review Press, 1997.

Yeager, Jeana and Dick Rutan with Phil Patton. *Voyager*. New York: Knopf, 1987.

Index

Bullard, Eugene, 38

155

156

husband), 76, 86
Marsh, Clara Jo, 119
The Messenger, 82, 83, 84
Mexico, 92
Midway Airport, 36
military aviation, women in, 15,
    106, 123, 124, 126-130, 145.
    See also Women's Air Force
    Service Pilots
Moisant, Alfred, 27-28
Moisant, John, 23, 27-28
Moisant, Matilde, 22, 23, 24, 26
Moisant International Aviators,
    23
Moisant School of Aviation, 23,
    24-25, 27
Mollison, Jim, 82, 83
monoplanes, 19, 27-28, 29, 89
Montijo, John "Monte," 56
Morrow, Dwight, 90, 91, 92, 99
Morse code, 93
Mount Zion Missionary Baptist
    Institutional Church, 47
Murphy, Sally, 128
Mussolini, Benito, 81

National Aerobatic
    Championship, 131, 133, 134
National Aeronautic
    Association, 56, 144
National Air and Space
    Museum, 134
National Airways, 65
National Aviation Hall of Fame,
    104, 122-123
National Geographic Society,
    61, 103-104
Navy, U.S., 112, 128-129, 130
Negro Welfare League, 48
New York Times, 24

Nichols, Ruth, 58
Nieuport Type 82 biplane, 40
Ninety-Nines, 58
Noonan, Fred, 67, 68, 69, 70
North to the Orient, 95

Odlum, Floyd, 110, 112, 114,
    122, 123
Orteig Prize, 90

Pacific Ocean, crossings of, by
    Earhart, 63-65, 71
Pan American Airways, 94, 101
Patty Wagstaff Airshows, 134
Paxon Field, 47, 48
Percival, Edgar, 83
Persian Gulf War, 129
Post Office, U.S., 33, 41
Presidential Citizens Award,
    144
Purdue Research Foundation,
    65
Purdue University, 65
Purves, Alexander "Jock," 76
Putnam, George Palmer, 56,
    57, 58-59, 60, 65-66, 114

Quimby, Harriet, 38, 145; death
    of, 32-33; early years of, 19-
    20; English Channel crossed
    by, 9, 28-31; flying costume
    of, 26, 27; flying lessons of,
    23, 24-25, 129; as journalist,
    8, 16, 20-21, 33; pilot's
    license earned by, 8-9, 17-19,
    25-26; as writer for *Leslie's
    Illustrated Weekly*, 9, 21-22,
    24, 26, 28
Quimby, Kitty (sister), 19, 20
Quimby, Ursula (mother), 19-

157

ABOUT THE AUTHOR

JACQUELINE McLEAN earned a doctorate in English Literature from New York University in May 1996. She writes frequently for young adults and children, as well as publishing poetry. Extraordinary women's stories are one of her passions. She currently teaches in the English department at Texas Tech University, where she is also employed as a book editor. She and the poet William Wenthe live in West Texas with their corgi, Edward, and cats, Spanky and Zero.

Photo Credits

Photographs courtesy of: cover (front top), pp. 6, 12, 16, 18, 22, 25, 30, 33, 34, 50, 55, 59, 62, 64, 66, 67, 96, 101, 103, 106, 113, National Air and Space Museum, Smithsonian Institution; cover (front bottom) and pp. 117, 119, 124, The Woman's Collection, Texas Woman's University; pp. 8, 14, 23, 27, 29, 52, 57, 70, 84, 87, 88, 91, 98, 100, 111, 116, 121, 123, Library of Congress; p. 10, Minnesota Historical Society; pp. 39, 42, Photograph and Prints Division, Schomburg Center for Research in Black Culture, The New York Public Library, Astor, Lenox and Tilden Foundations; p. 45, Glenn Curtiss Museum, Hammondsport, N.Y.; p. 46, The Black Film Center/Archive, Indiana University, Bloomington, Ind.; p. 49, Eartha M. M. White Collection, Thomas G. Carpenter Library, University of North Florida; p. 72, Popperfoto/Archive Photos; pp. 74, 86, 105, 139, 144, AP/Wide World Photos; p. 77, Illustrated London News/Archive Photos; p. 127, National Archives; p. 130, Defense Visual Information Center; pp. 132, 135, and cover (back), Patty Wagstaff Airshows.